The Wise Investor

Ten Concepts You Need to Know to Achieve Financial Success

Neil Elmouchi
with
Leonard M. Coris

SPECIAL EDITION

Dunhill & West Publishing
Westlake Village, California 91362

THE WISE INVESTOR

Ten Concepts You Need To Know To Achieve Financial Success

By Neil Elmouchi, ChFC

Published by:
Dunhill & West Publishing
P.O. Box 32
Agoura, CA 91376

Printed in the United States of America
10 9 8 7 6 5 4 3 2

Library of Congress Catalog Number: 96-93002
ISBN: 0-9654215-0-3

Book Design and Typography by ONE-ON-ONE Book Production

Cover Design by Joe Cibere

What Others Are Saying about this Book

"This is by far one of the best books I have read on financial concepts. This should be first on your reading list of investment books. Don't let the simplicity of the book's style and its ease of reading mislead you—it contains the fundamental concepts we all need to understand in order to achieve financial success. These concepts are so important I recommend re-reading this book at least once a year."
—Don Ogilvie, President Olgivie Security Advisors Corp.

"This is no ordinary text book. It contains valuable information that is relevant to any financial strategy. The book is easy to read and points out critical concepts for developing one's financial success."
—David Hartman, Certified Public Accountant

"If I would have understood the concepts in this book when I was in my 20's, I could have been financially secure in my 40's. Even though I didn't start investing until I was older, I am going to make sure my children understand the importance of starting their financial planning now. I want each of them to read this book."
—George Bloom, Screen & Television Writer

"I am giving a copy of this book to each of my children. This book is a perfect way for them to start to appreciate the value of investing money and preparing for their future."
—Mort Scolnick, Real Estate Developer

"Read this book if you want to make sure you are on the right investment path. It's fun to read and the concepts are explained in an easy to understand format. I am recommending it to all of my clients."
—Randee B. Held, Certified Financial Planner

Warning - Disclaimer

This book is designed to provide information in regards to the subject matter covered. It is sold with the understanding that the publisher and authors are not engaged in rendering legal or accounting services nor is this book intended to replace other professional services. If legal, financial or other expert assistance is required, the services of a competent professional should be sought.

It is not the purpose of this book to reprint all the information that is otherwise available to the author and/or publisher, but to complement, amplify and supplement other texts. You are encouraged to read all the available material, learn as much as possible about investing and financial planning and to tailor the information to your individual needs. For more information, see recommended reading in the Appendix.

Every effort has been made to make this book as complete and as accurate as possible. However, there may be mistakes both typographical and in content. Therefore, this text should be used only as a general guide and not as the ultimate source of investing and financial planning information.

The purpose of this book is to educate and provide the information in an entertaining fashion. The author and Dunhill & West Publishing shall have neither liability nor responsibility to any person or entity with respect to any loss or damage caused, or alleged to be caused, directly or indirectly by the information contained in this book.

Acknowledgment

We would like to show our appreciation and give special thanks to a number of people that provided invaluable assistance in the editing of this book. We sincerely wish to thank all these fine people:

Lawrence N.Berke	First Vice President, First of Michigan Corp.
George Arthur Bloom	Screen & Television Writer
Harold Brooks	Vice President, Windsor Insurance Associates, Inc.
Charles Ferrone	Principal of Watermill Financial Group
Timothy Fitch	Vice President, ITT Hartford Life Insurance
Barry Harlan	Attorney, Certified Family Law Specialist
David A. Hartman	Certified Public Accountant
Randee B. Held	Certified Financial Planner
David Isaacson	Watermill Financial Group
Barry Lefkowitz	Certified Public Accountant
Robert Melcher	Business & Tax Accountant
Richard Moss	Attorney
Don Ogilvie	President, Ogilvie Security Advisors Corp.
Jerry Orefice	Estate Planner
Jim Richman	Corporate President
Karna Schafer	Property Development
Marc Schwartz	Vice President, Windsor Insurance Associates, Inc.
Mort Scolnick	Real Estate Developer
Carl Sternberg	Chartered Financial Consultant
Lewis Thomashow	Certified Public Accountant
Peter Wakeman	Estate, & Tax Attorney
Anne Westrope	Vice President, Bachrach & Associates

SPECIAL THANKS

Special thanks should go to our office staff members: Josephine Smith, Lynn Cornejo and Betti Hendrickson, for their help with the development and editing of this book.

About Neil Elmouchi, ChFC

A financial strategist with extensive experience in investments, tax planning, wealth conservation and risk management, Neil Elmouchi is President of Westlake Village, California-based Summit Consultants & Financial Services, Inc. Active in the financial services industry since 1969, Mr. Elmouchi's background includes being an agency Vice President for one of the nation's largest financial and insurance companies before establishing his financial management firm in 1985.

Mr. Elmouchi received his bachelor's degree in business administration from Wayne State University in Detroit, MI. He holds the designations of ChFC (Chartered Financial Consultant) and CLU (Chartered Life Underwriter); and he is a member of the Million Dollar Roundtable, the American Society of CLU's and ChFC's, and the President's Advisory Council of the City of Hope.

In his work, Mr Elmouchi frequently provides counsel to other financial planners, as well as attorneys and accountants, in cases requiring his advanced technical expertise. His financial background includes teaching courses in economics, business insurance and accounting for the American College and conducting money management seminars for companies such as Dole Foods, AutoLogic, and PTI Technologies.

Specializing in working with high net worth individuals, successful professionals and owners of closely-held corporations, he designs and implements investment strategies that allow his clients to chart a course toward their financial security. His firm is proud of its excellent reputation and prides itself in developing long-term relationships with its clients.

About Leonard M. Coris, CLU, ChFC

Leonard M. Coris founded Watermill Financial Group in1968. He received his Master's Degree in Finance from the M.I.T. Sloan School of Management in 1970, and was one of the first to earn both an M.S. in Financial Services and a Chartered Financial Consultant (ChFC) designation from the American College, Bryn Mawr, PA. Mr. Coris is also a Chartered Life Underwriter (CLU), a Registered Health Underwriter (RHU), and a licensed Life and Health Insurance Advisor.

Leonard Coris has been providing personal benefit programs for more than 30 years. He is the president of Watermill Advisory Services, Inc., an Investment Advisory firm. Mr. Coris is also licensed to sell securities through Royal Alliance Associates, Inc., a national independent registered broker-dealer.

Leonard Coris who is listed in *Who's Who in American Finance*, has been very active in the local Estate and Business Planning Councils in both Boston and Tucson, and is a member of several professional organizations including the International Association for Financial Planners and the American Society of CLU's and ChFC's. His professional accomplishments include numerous awards and designations as well as selection for membership in the prestigious Association for Advanced Life Underwriters, the International Forum and the Top of the Table.

Table of Contents

Dedication

I would like to dedicate this book to my wife, Doris and daughters, Lisa and Julie for their encouragement and support and to my clients, who have been crucial to the development and success of Watermill Financial Group.

Introduction

My clients are successful business people, professionals and entrepreneurs who have become aware of the need for both retirement and estate planning. They have a need to understand both the problems and solutions involved in the process of accumulating, retaining and controlling the disposition of assets, with some control of the tax impact. In addition, they require both prompt and accurate responses to their questions and concerns. However, as competent as they are in their own professions, most have neither the perspective nor the education and training that is necessary to optimize both the growth and preservation of their assets.

Personal financial and estate planning issues generally affect the entire future financial security of my clients and their families. Therefore, we believe that it is vital for people to be able to make informed decisions in the evaluation and selection of both their advisors and planning vehicles.

In order for you to attain financial security, you ultimately need a plan that is tailored to your personal needs and goals. It is necessary to create a team of professional advisors with diverse expertise and experience in a number of related disciplines, selecting one member of the team to be responsible for coordinating the process. Proper financial and estate planning can help you reach a balance between the accumulation of wealth and the specific on-going needs of your family.

You should be involved in structuring this necessary planning process for your self and your family. With a reasonable introduction to certain financial concepts, and your own good judgment in the selection of advisors, this important process can be completed without undue stress.

The Wise Investor straightforwardly presents a breadth of inforation that we have rarely found in any other single publication. It is an excellent primer on financial concepts for intelligent people who have a wide range of business and investment experience. Reading this concise book will introduce you to many of the concepts and concerns which are involved in the design and implementation of a personal financial and estate plan. It will also provide a basis for developing a relevant strategy with the team of advisors, which you select. It is one step in the process of better understanding your personal financial needs and what you have to do to attain them.

If you understand the conceptual foundation for the creation and management of wealth that is presented in this book, you will be better able to understand and implement a meaningful personal program. You will have taken positive steps toward becoming a *wise investor* yourself.

1

How Will You Know When Opportunity is Knocking if You're Not Listening?

> *"If you don't know where you are going, how will you know when you get there?"*
> —**Anonymous**

66 The harder you work, the luckier you get." I have heard this statement thousands of times and I believe it to be true. But over the years I've heard another statement that I do *not* believe is true, "Opportunity only knocks once." I have found quite the opposite to be true: *Opportunity is continually knocking, you just have to know how to open the door.* In other words, opportunities are always around us, the riches

of the world are at our feet, but only if we are able to hear the "call," open our eyes and clearly see the wealth that lies before us.

"Opportunity" is just another word for choices. Every day we are confronted with numerous choices. Some choices are important and some are inconsequential. But that does not change the fact that each choice we make harbors a potential opportunity. Being able to identify and then take advantage of these opportunities is the challenge.

> *"Opportunity is continually knocking, you just have to know how to open the door."*
> —**Neil Elmouchi**

How do you know if opportunity is staring you in the face? How do you know if your eyes are open? You must start with a clear picture of what you want to accomplish. The only way to bring this picture into focus is to have a plan. A financial plan will chart your course, it will guide your progress, and it will let you know when you have reached your destination. A plan will enhance your ability to identify and grasp an opportunity when it knocks. This book will describe the critical concepts necessary to establish an effective financial plan.

Making the Commitment . . .

Sarah Barnes has worked at Intercorp Communications for ten years and is now senior vice president of the marketing division. She has over twenty years experience in the industry and is respected among her co-workers for her organizational talents. She has a logical mind and tries to evaluate all of her options before making important decisions. While Sarah's job can be demanding, she has always been up front with her employer about what her priorities are—her family comes first. Sarah does an excellent job of leaving the work-related stress at the office so she can give her family and herself quality time.

Her husband, Jim, is a partner in a small printing company. He makes a good income, but their lifestyle requires both of their incomes to make ends meet. Like Sarah, he too has made the commitment that their family comes first. Together they work to provide a quality homelife. They respect each other's busy schedules so they do their best to share the household responsibilities and take care of their two children; Darryl, an energetic eleven-year-old and Kimberly, who just had her ninth birthday.

Jim just turned forty-eight years old, and Sarah is approaching her forty-fifth birthday. For some reason this birthday is causing Sarah to think more about their financial future. Together, they have recently started talking about how they are going to pay for their children's' college education and realize that they should also start planning for their retirement.

During a typical workweek at Intercorp, Sarah was normally very focused on the current projects for which she is responsible. But by the end of this particular workday, her attention had taken another direction. In fact, when Pete Hadley poked his head in her office to say "goodnight," it was obvious to him that Sarah was concentrating her energies on something important.

Sarah is Pete's boss. They have worked together for the past seven years at Intercorp. Pete is the marketing division's Senior Account Executive. He is a good salesman, but doesn't like to get bogged down in detail work. Like many good salespeople, he is always focused on closing the next deal and wants to leave the specifics to the rest of his team. Pete is forty-one years old and married to Marie, his wife of eleven years. Marie is thrity-nine years old. They have three children, ages three, six and eight.

It had been a hectic day for Pete. It was 5:30 and he was very glad this workday had come to an end. "Hi Sarah, what are you up to?" Pete said as he stuck his head into Sarah's office. "Putting together my financial plan," Sarah answered, her eyes glued to the computer screen. "I've been promising myself I would start one but I never seem to get around to it."

"I put my plan together a couple of years ago," Pete boasted. "Did the whole thing in one day. If you need any help with yours, I'd be happy to lend a hand."

"You know, Pete, I would be interested in your opinion," Sarah replied. "I have a few questions that I've been trying to answer for myself."

Pete sat himself in front of Sarah's desk. "Fire away."

"Well, the first question I'm trying to answer is: How much money will we need to live on when we're retired?" Sarah asked. "What did you come up with?"

"Gee, I'm not sure." Pete replied. "I didn't think about that when I did my plan."

"Well, how did you calculate how much money you would need at retirement?"

"Oh, it wasn't that complicated," Pete answered. "In my plan, I just decided to invest in the company's 401k and put a couple hundred a month into mutual funds until I retired."

Sarah tried not to show her astonishment, "So you don't actually have a specific dollar amount you're trying to accumulate?"

"Well, no, I figured I'm putting away enough money. It's sure to be enough by the time I reach sixty-five." Pete said, a little defensive. "Heck, remember Roger Stewart?"

"Yes."

"Well, I talked to him just before he retired, and he told me that his 401k would give him a big chunk of his retirement income. He said it earned him a great deal of money. I figure mine will do the same."

"Did you ask him which mutual funds he invested in or what he considered a great deal of money or what his strategy was?" Sarah asked.

"Not exactly, but I think he invested into a number of those stock-type mutual funds. Why?"

"Well, I wondered if you followed his investment strategy or did something else."

"The truth is, Sarah, I am a little scared of stocks," Pete replied. "You know those things can go up in value—but they can go down too. They can be pretty risky. So I put half of my money in the money market and half in a bond fund. You don't make as much that way, but I feel safer

"So, how often do you check on the performance of your investments?" Sarah asked.

"That's the great thing about my plan," Pete replied. "It's so simple, I don't have to do much. Actually, I haven't had the time to see how it's doing. I get so wrapped up with work and the family...but your right. I should take a look at my investments soon."

Sarah took a deep breath. "So," she said, trying not to sound too critical, "your plan is to put your money into investments that typically bring a lower rate of return, in order to accumulate an undecided amount of money. And, you don't regularly monitor your progress to see if you're on target for your goals, which you really don't have a clear picture of in the first place?"

"Hey, it's not *that* bad." Pete retorted. "I think it's pretty good for someone who's not a regular investor. What's going to make your plan any better? Neither one of us are Wall Street wizards."

> *"When you have to make a choice and don't make it, that is in itself a choice."*
> —**William James**

"That's true, Pete. But I recently went to a management seminar regarding the importance of writing a business plan for our company. The speaker talked about how a business plan is the first step to getting control of your future.

"It got me thinking about long-term planning. The same process applies to personal financial planning. His talk covered points I'd heard a thousand times before, but for some reason, this time I truly saw their value. I don't know if it's because I am getting older, and maybe a little wiser or that I just want to start to take control of my future. Whatever the reason, I've made a personal commitment to put my own plan together."

Pete agreed. "That makes sense but why does it have to be complicated?"

"Well, the seminar leader gave an interesting example about the importance of having a clear picture of what you want to accomplish."

"And what was that?" Pete wanted to know.

"He explained that a plane flying from Los Angeles to Honolulu is off course over 90 percent of the time."

"How can that be?" Pete asked.

"There are lots of reasons: atmospheric conditions, winds, you name it. What's important is not that the plane is off course, but that the pilot knows where he is headed. As long as he knows where he wants to go, all he has to do is monitor his progress and make course corrections whenever the plane strays from the charted course."

"But, how does that apply to financial planning?"

"The point is," Sarah replied, "you may think you are saving large sums of money, but you'll have no idea if it will be enough until it's too late to do anything about it. If you don't know how much you will need, how will you know if you have enough?"

Pete nodded his head. "I see your point."

"By the way, Pete. Do you know what it's called when an airline pilot makes course corrections?"

"No."

"He's changing the plane's *attitude*," Sarah said with a smile. "So I decided to write a plan that helps me adjust *my attitude* as conditions change."

"How are you going to do that?"

"I'm not exactly sure but I've got an idea. I'm going to talk to a friend of mine who once mentioned to me that he wrote a financial plan. I think you know him—Joe Franklin. He owns a chain of furniture stores and he has been very successful in his business and handling his finances. He has three kids, and the oldest is in college right now. Laura, his wife, says they are thinking about retiring in the next few years even though he is only fifty-one years old.

"We're getting together for lunch this Saturday so I can ask him how he drafted his financial plan. In fact, Joe really peaked my interest during our last phone conversation when he said he would tell me the secrets he learned on how to become financially independent. Would you like to join us?"

"Well, a comment like that would spark my interest to," Pete replied. "I'd love to join you, if it's okay with Joe. Call me when you know the time we'll meet and I'll drive."

> *"You cannot control the wind; but you can direct the sails... "*
>
> **—Anonymous**

2

Is this Picture a Little Fuzzy... or do I Need Glasses?

> *"Common sense is not so common"*
> —Voltaire

Pete spent Saturday morning gardening in the yard, then he cleaned up before heading over to pick up Sarah for the ride to the restaurant.

"So, where are we headed for lunch?" Pete asked.

"Houston's," Sarah replied. "Joe's always talking about how great it is, and I've never been there, so I figured we could give it a try."

"Sounds good to me."

Sarah and Pete arrived at the restaurant first and settled into a booth near the window. Soon they saw Joe pull up in front of the restaurant. He hopped out of his car and headed into the restaurant, looking tan and fit.

"Success sure agrees with him, doesn't it?" Pete remarked to Sarah as Joe headed across the restaurant toward their table.

"Yeah, it sure does."

"Hi Sarah!" Joe called out as he approached the table. "Great to see you!"

"Likewise!" replied Sarah. "Do you remember Pete Hadley? We work together at Intercorp."

"Sure do!" said Joe. "Nice to see you again."

The three caught up on news about their families and work. They ordered lunch as they chatted. After the waiter brought their entrees, the conversation started to get down to the business at hand. Sarah started, "Joe, a long time ago you mentioned that you wrote a financial plan. What convinced you to put a plan together in the first place?"

"Focus," Joe replied simply.

"Focus?" Sarah and Pete said together.

Joe continued. "In business, you have to have a clear picture of what you want to achieve, and a plan is the best way I know to accomplish that. You know, I don't think I know a single *really* successful business owner who operates without a plan.

"So, it just seemed natural to apply that thinking to my personal financial goals

"But running a business and doing financial planning are two different things," protested Pete. "I don't see how..."

"Are they *really* that different?" Joe interrupted. "Think about it. You have hopes and aspirations for your family, just as you do for your career. You want to do a good job raising your kids, putting them through college, perhaps buying a second home or traveling or retiring early. Your list may be different from my list, but you have goals you want to achieve, just like I do. That's just like having a business plan—having a list of goals you'd like to achieve."

> *"A definite goal and a specific deadline—these are the keys to achieving one's destiny."*
> **—Anonymous**

Pete had to agree with him. "I suppose."

"Until you apply some of the principles of a business plan to your personal financial plan, most of what you wish for will remain just that—a wish. But if you focus on your wishes, and identify what you have to do to attain them, you may see them come true."

"Sounds sensible to me," Sarah agreed.

Joe continued. "I call it my 'Strategic Life Plan,' because it's much more than a financial plan If you decide to write your own plan you will soon discover that it can have a positive impact on your *whole life*, not just your *finances*."

"I believe what you are saying in principle," Pete said, "but it's still hard for me to believe that *whatever* I dream can come true. Especially given what I make and what it costs to live these days."

"Well, I'll tell you, Pete," Joe replied, "over the years, I've seen virtually every dream that was really important to me come true, or is well on the way to becoming true. It's all because those dreams were part of my Strategic Life Plan. In other words, my Strategic Life Plan helped me turn my dreams into reality."

"Can't the plan become kind of limiting?" Pete asked. "What happens if you're presented with an opportunity you hadn't considered? If it doesn't fit into your plan, what do you do?"

"Nothing is cast in stone," Joe replied. "I've made a number of changes to my financial plan over the years, but I think long and hard every time I change the plan. We're all tempted to do things that affect our finances, whether it is buying a new car, or purchasing a house that's really out of your price range, or getting involved in a new get-rich-quick scheme. It's easy to find new ways to spend your money.

"You must give careful consideration to each new opportunity that arises before you make any changes. Don't just look at the opportunity by itself. Make sure to evaluate its effect on your overall financial plan.

"Some of the initial goals I set out in my first plan aren't there anymore," Joe added. "I've accomplished some of them and I've lost interest in others. I've added some new goals. But all in all, having the plan has meant all the difference."

> *"Well done is better than well said."*
> **—Ben Franklin**

"Joe, you're pretty passionate about this financial planning stuff, excuse me, 'Strategic Life Plan'!" laughed Sarah. "You've made a believer out of me! How do I get started?"

Joe laughed as well. "Well Sarah, I didn't mean to go overboard, but I really do owe whatever financial success I have to my plan."

"OK, you've got me hooked too!" declared Pete. "So how did you decide what to put into your plan?"

"I *didn't* decide," answered Joe. "I was no more certain of what belonged in my plan than you are right now."

"But you did your own plan!" argued Pete.

"No, I decided that I *needed* my own plan. But I soon discovered something very important."

"What was that?" Sarah wanted to know.

"I realized that there was a lot more to learn about writing a plan than just putting a few thoughts down on a piece of paper," Joe answered. "You need to appreciate the difference between understanding the concepts and implementing the details. There are certain concepts you need to have a clear understanding of *and* you need to know how to apply them. They are critical to the development and success of your plan."

"So *what are* these concepts?" Pete asked a bit impatiently.

"They are the key to your future." Joe said rather mysteriously. "But before I tell you about the concepts I need to explain one other thing first."

"Which is...?" Sarah prodded.

"The difference between *concepts* and *details*," Joe answered.

"Well, explain away!" Pete said enthusiastically.

> *"We grow old too soon and smart too late."*
> —Paraphrase of an Old Pennsylvania Dutch saying

> "*Experience is the dividend you get from your mistakes.*"
>
> —Anonymous

> "*There is only one class in the community that thinks more about money than the rich, and that is the poor. The poor can think of nothing else.*"
>
> —Oscar Wilde

3

What do You Mean
I don't Know
My Concepts from
My Details?!

> *"Without a conceptual framework, there is no plan. With one, you have the structure for your specific financial decisions."*
>
> —Neil Elmouchi

"Before I start, why don't we take advantage of this beautiful day and continue the discussion in the park across the street?" Joe suggested.

"Great idea," agreed Sarah.

They finished their coffee and headed outside.

Sarah pointed to a shady spot across the street. "There are some tables and benches under the tree. How about sitting over there and we can talk some more?"

"Looks like a good place to me," said Joe.

The threesome crossed the street and headed into the city park. They seated themselves at a table under the shade tree. Pete resumed the conversation. "So what's the difference between concepts and details?"

"That's the next point I want to talk about," replied Joe. "However, the explanation may take a little time. Do either of you have to leave soon?"

"No, my afternoon is open if yours is," said Pete. Sarah nodded in agreement. "Good," said Joe. "Let's begin with a discussion about *concepts*. At this stage they are more important to you than details."

Somewhat puzzled, Pete interjected, "Joe, aren't the *details* what makes your plan really work for you?"

"Well, yes," agreed Joe, "but that's why it's important to understand the difference between the two." "It doesn't help to talk about the details of *my* specific goals, if my goals aren't the same as *yours*. But it *does* help to talk about how I went about setting those goals, and the *concepts* I used to guide my thinking."

"Well, if a financial plan is so personal, can the concepts be all that consistent? Why wouldn't they be different for everyone, just like the details?" Sarah asked.

"You use the concepts to *develop* your financial plan," replied Joe. "Without a conceptual framework, there *is* no plan. With one, you have the structure for your specific financial decisions."

"You're still talking Greek," laughed Pete.

Joe grinned. "I know, I had the same problem when I first heard this idea. Let me give you the example that my financial advisor gave me. He said, 'Knowing that your car should have regular oil changes doesn't mean that you have to change the oil yourself.' In other words, I needed to understand the *concept* of oil changes. I had to recognize that it is a valuable thing to do every three or four thousand miles in order to keep my car running right and avoid mechanical problems. But I *don't* need to know the details, I *don't* need to *know how* to change the oil. That's why I have a mechanic!

Pete and Sarah nodded. Things were becoming clearer now. Joe continued "It's the same with my Strategic Life Plan. If I understand the concepts on which my planning decisions should be based, I can rely on the appropriate professional—my accountant, attorney or financial advisor—to make specific legal, financial or investment decisions that mesh with these concepts. Each of these advisors has an expertise that I can draw upon as needed.

"I have to put things in the right perspective. I'm not a financial expert, I'm the owner of a chain of furniture stores, I know what I do well, and that is selling furniture and working with customers. And I know what to do when I *don't* do something well, I hire someone who does."

"Okay, you've made some very good points about learning concepts. So how many of them are there?" Sarah asked.

"There are ten fundamental concepts," Joe replied. "Ten concepts you need to understand before you start your plan or invest a dime."

"So, just what are those magical concepts?" Sarah asked. "What do we have to understand to develop a financial plan?"

"I brought along copies of the list of concepts my financial planner gave me at our first meeting," Joe handed Sarah and Pete each a copy of the list. "These are the concepts behind an effective financial plan. Take a look."

The list intrigued Sarah and Pete.

"The only thing more expensive than education is ignorance."

—**Anonymous**

Ten Fundamental Concepts for Establishing a Sound Financial Strategy

1. Information is NOT Necessarily Knowledge.

2. Why Olympic Athletes Have Coaches.

3. Understanding Your Most Valuable Asset.

4. The Difference between Wants and Likes.

5. Establishing the Long-Term Perspective.

6. Never Gamble with Your Future.

7. The Only Guarantee in Life is that Everything Involves Risk.

8. Are You a Lender or an Investor?

9. Know the Rules Before You Play the Game

10. If I Tell You Where It Hurts, Do I Still Have to Pay You?

"Before I explain the concepts, I want to tell you what my advisor told me when we were getting started," Joe continued. "He explained that while he could help me identify and work toward specific *financial* goals, it was up to me to clarify and prioritize my *personal* goals."

"*Personal* goals?" Pete interjected. "I thought we were talking about financial planning and investments."

"You're right, Pete," Joe replied, "but you will soon discover as I did that personal goals will have a direct influence on how you put together your plan. That's why he wanted me to understand the areas his expertise could guide me through and those areas that were up to me. He couldn't tell me, for example, how much time I should spend with my family, what special things I'd like to do for my kids; the dreams Laura and I should have for our future; or how important exercise, diet or relaxation are to me; or how I'd like to fulfill my spiritual needs. All of these items are part of my Strategic Life Plan, and they are *all* affected by my financial security."

"Sounds like your financial planner doubles as a personal guru," joked Pete.

"Well, he sure helped me figure out what was really important to me and what wasn't. He wanted to make sure that I shared my thoughts with my wife, and my children, if they were old enough; instead of assuming they knew what I was thinking. And you know, he was absolutely right. It's just like in business, when everyone in the company has a clear vision of what the company is trying to accomplish, getting there is a lot smoother."

"It's the same for your family. If you know what you are trying to achieve five or ten years from now, it is much easier *not* to spend money on something right now if spending that money will make it harder to reach your goal. You will be able to differentiate between what is truly important and what is a spur-of-the-moment emotional reaction."

Joe paused for a few seconds and looked at the expressions on Sarah and Pete's faces, then continued, "I hope this makes sense to you. Are you ready to hear about the concepts?"

"You've got my attention!" declared Sarah. "Start explaining!"

"Yes!" agreed Pete. "I want to know all about each concept."

"OK," replied Joe. "Let's take the concepts one at a time."

> *"Nothing ever becomes real 'till it is experienced."*
> —**John Keats**

> *"We do not need to know how we're actually going to achieve a goal when we set it. Just repeatedly visualize the desired end result, and the how will open up."*

> *"Because We Can —We Do*
> *Because We Do—We Expect*
> *Because We Expect — We Can."*
> —Neil Elmouchi

4

Information is NOT Necessarily Knowledge

> *"The information supply available to us doubles every five years."*
>
> —Richard Saul Wurman,
> author, *Information Anxiety*

"OK. Number one: why isn't information the same as knowledge?" asked Sarah.

"And," chimed in Pete, "what does the difference have to do with putting together a financial plan?"

"When my advisor first gave me the 'information isn't knowledge' speech, I asked the same questions." Joe replied.

"Now, I don't think I could tell you which of the ten concepts is more important than the other, but I can tell you that I think this one is the most fascinating.

Sarah and Pete looked at each other, intrigued. Joe continued. "Think about the pace of technology. It's clear that we will most likely experience more technological breakthroughs in the first twenty years of the Twenty-first Century than we did throughout the entire Twentieth Century. And if we look at how technology has already impacted our lives, it becomes clear that these breakthroughs have not necessarily *simplified* things. Instead we are moving faster than ever before; asking new questions, and seeking more answers. If anything, new technology is adding *pressure* to our lives!"

> *"You'er in Paris. And you decided to use your American Express card. Getting the credit approval involves a 46,000-mile journey over phones and computers. The job can be completed in five seconds.*
>
> —Peter Large

"You know, when Lincoln was President, it would have taken us over two months to travel from England to California. If you were in Los Angeles and wanted to communicate with someone in London, it could take weeks. How long are we willing to wait for a response from a company in England today? How long are we willing to wait to find out if a product manufactured in England is available for shipping?"

"If I need it," Sarah answered, "I want to know today."

"Right," agreed Pete. "I'd probably fax or E-mail them and ask for a response by the end of the day."

"And would you want it shipped tomorrow?" Joe asked.

"Of course!" both Sarah and Pete replied.

"Think about how quickly that information went back and forth," Joe said. "You had instant access to it, right?"

"Right," Pete and Sarah agreed.

"Okay. Here's the fascinating part: Does having that information mean that you've increased your level of *knowledge*?" questioned Joe.

"Well..." Sarah said slowly, "I'm not sure... if I knew a product was available right away."

"Yes, that's *information*," Joe said. "But is it *knowledge*? Can you really equate the two? What I've learned is that information and knowledge are related, but they are not the same. All of the information that is at our disposal right now, and all of the new information that will come in the next century won't make us more knowledgeable. It will just mean that we have access to more information!"

"We already have so many ways to access it," Sarah pointed out. "Books, newspapers, magazines, TV news, newsletters, radio, the Internet..."

"That's right," Joe agreed. "That's right. You already have instant access to information on just about any topic you can imagine. Surf the Internet, pick a topic, and you will have hundreds or even thousands of articles, books and experts available to give you information. But can you *absorb* all that information?"

"Not all of it," replied Pete.

"So if you can't absorb all that information, is it knowledge?" asked Joe. "Not really," answered Pete. "So if we can't absorb all the information, what good is it to us?"

> *"Information is merely a bunch of facts and figures; it only becomes valuable knowledge when someone filters it in a meaningful way."*
> **—Neil Elmouchi**

"Well, having access to information is good," Joe answered. "That kind of access creates opportunities to grow, to widen your horizons. Because there is so much information at your fingertips, you've got to start distinguishing between the information that can build your knowledge base and the information that you can't act on."

"What do you mean?" Sarah asked. "If I get some information and I understand it, why can't I act on it?"

"Well," replied Joe, "information is just a set of facts, figures, and data that can be very interesting but also completely meaningless if you don't have a way to understand it and *use* it. You can get information on just about anything: baking a cake, brain surgery, building an atom bomb. That doesn't mean you could personally put that information to work. Knowing how to effectively *apply* what you've learned is what turns information into *knowledge*. *You have to know how to use it* and if you don't know, you have to find someone who does.

"Sarah and Pete were a bit confused at this point.

Joe continued. "Consider this example. If someone in your family needed heart bypass surgery, you could easily locate all of the information about bypass surgery. You could read the medical texts and get detailed instructions on how heart bypass surgery is performed. You could look at diagrams, photos and X-rays. Just flip the switch on your computer and instantly be able cruise the Internet for what you need, hit a couple of keys, and download. You've got all of the information you would ever want on bypass surgery right there at your fingertips. So why not save the money and hassle, and do the surgery yourself? You've got all that information."

"But I don't know how to use it," Sarah replied. "I don't have the experience!"

"Precisely!" Joe grinned, knowing he'd made his point. "You don't just need *information*, you also need *experience*. You need training and education to take that information, those facts, and put them to good use. All of those factors start to change information into knowledge."

"But there are many subjects that we could gather information on and use ourselves," interrupted Sarah. "There are times when we could use it without having prior experience."

"Sure," agreed Joe, "but that's usually true in cases where making a wrong decision won't have a huge negative impact on your life. Maybe you can use the information to decide which brand of TV to buy or where to go on your next vacation. Your life won't be altered terribly if you make a wrong decision in those instances.

"But what if a wrong decision means you don't get the medical care you need, or you run out of retirement funds before you run out of years? Those are the kinds of situations where you should let a professional lead the way in putting all that information to work for you."

"Won't I be a better consumer of a professional's services if I read up on the information that is available?" asked Pete.

"Of course," replied Joe. "Information can be very valuable, even if you need a professional's help to act on it. You must keep in mind that information is merely a bunch of facts and figures, and it only becomes valuable knowledge when someone filters it in a meaningful way."

"In other words," Sarah cut in, "you should have the background, training and experience to determine which information is appropriate for a given situation. Only then can the information be considered knowledge. And if I don't already have the expertise to effectively convert that information into knowledge, I should use a professional who can make sure the job is done right."

"Exactly!" smiled Joe. "You've got the first concept. Focus your energies on what *you* do best and hire professionals for what *they* do best."

> *"A little knowledge that acts is worth infinitely more than much knowledge that is idle."*
>
> —Kahlil Gibran

> *"Between us, we cover all knowledge; he knows all that can be known and I know the rest."*
>
> — Mark Twain

5

Why
Olympic Athletes
Have Coaches

> *"If you keep thinking that you can do it all yourself, you are going to be very stressed as society becomes more complex and fast-paced."*
> —Neil Elmouchi

"OK, now we're rolling," said Sarah. "Let's get into concept number two!"

"Yes," agreed Pete. "I have some ideas of my own about why Olympic athletes have coaches, but I'd sure like to hear what your financial buddy has to say on the subject."

"Well," said Joe, "this one flows pretty logically from the first concept. It ties together the issues of time, information overload and skills. We are talking about focusing on *your* strengths and effectively using the strengths of others.

"If you think," Joe continued, "about the fact that we can ask questions, get information, and act on that information in minutes or hours instead of days or weeks, you start to see why we must do more, think faster, and make critical decisions quicker than we ever had to before. So we have less time to evaluate information and less time to consider all of the variables of a particular decision."

"That's true," Sarah declared. "It's really hard to keep up sometimes. There have been plenty of times when I've wondered if I'm competent to handle a decision, because I have so little time to really think it through."

"I make the best decision I can, given the amount of time I have," said Pete. "But, I can't quite see what this has to do with coaches."

"It's about delegation," Joe replied.

"Delegation?" Pete echoed.

"Right. In theory, delegating is easy, but in reality it's hard for most people. However, it's an important part of making good decisions."

"How?" Sarah asked.

"Well, everyone has some unique talent, something that they are very good at doing. It's the most important skill they bring to whatever they do. It might be designing, writing, selling, research, administration or computer skills—whatever. Your unique talent is your strength, and you become most productive when you're doing something that draws on that talent. Likewise, you're less productive when you're trying to do something you may be capable of doing, but it's not really one of your strengths.

"For most of us," Joe continued, "our talent is *not* synonymous with our total job. It's usually just one aspect of the job. So if we're going to be effective, our goal has to be the elimination of activities that distract us from focusing our energies on what we do best. We've got to focus on our strengths, and delegate everything else."

> *"Getting something done is an accomplishment; getting something done right is an achievement."*
> —Anonymous

"There's no way I could delegate everything I don't want to do," protested Sarah.

"Probably not," Joe agreed. "But you can delegate some things, and probably more than you think. If you keep thinking that you can do it all yourself, you are going to be very stressed as society becomes more complex and fast-paced. We all have to change our mindset and make a paradigm shift in the way we approach the things we do. We have to ask ourselves, 'What do I do best?' What if I focused my energies on my strengths, those talents I excel at, and delegate the rest of my responsibilities to other people? What would that do to my life?"

"What do you mean, 'What would that do to my life?'" asked Sarah.

"Well, would you have more freedom? Would you have more time for your family? Would you enjoy life more? Would it improve the quality of your life? Would you be more productive? Would you make more money? Would it be worth doing?" Joe challenged.

"Sure," Sarah said, "probably all of those things."

"Well, this concept is about identifying the things you currently do but could be done better by someone else. It doesn't have to be something major or life-threatening. Start with the little things."

"How about mowing my lawn and doing yard work?" Pete interrupted. "I spend almost half a day every weekend in the yard, I suppose I could hire someone to do it for me. It's just been part of my routine for so long that I never took the time to question whether it's something I should be doing. Delegating that job would sure make my life more enjoyable!"

"That's exactly what I mean, Pete," Joe said enthusiastically. "What about you, Sarah?"

"The first thing I thought about is my weekly production report. I'm required to prepare the report every week for management. It takes a ton of time and I hate doing it. Now that I think about it, the only reason I keep doing it is because I've always done it. My assistant, Brian, has all of the data in his computer, and he likes detail work a lot more than I do. I'm going to delegate that job to him. You know, I feel better already!"

"OK," interrupted Pete, "the concept of delegation is great. What does it have to do with investment strategies and my personal plan?"

"Everything," answered Joe, "because it points out a fatal flaw in the perception of ourselves—a flaw that will cause us all kinds of problems in the Information Age. The flaw is based on the underlying assumption that we can and should be able to do everything ourselves. Partially researching a topic can be very dangerous. It can give a false sense of security about your ability in an area that could be more complex than it first appears. For example, just because we have access to a vast amount of investment data, does not automatically give you or me the appropriate expertise to make critical decisions about our financial future."

"Back to the idea of information versus knowledge," Sarah remarked.

"Right," Joe said. "Which leads us into the discussion about why an Olympic athlete needs a coach."

"This is a good question," said Pete. "It would seem logical, that if they had the talent, they could do it all themselves. Why can't they just train themselves?"

"If someone wants to become a world class athlete," Joe responded, "they need to focus their energies on what they do best, they have to be single-minded. Just because someone is a natural runner, does not mean that they know the best running techniques, or the best training methods, or that they understand all the competitive strategies of the sport. They obtain that information from the experts. They need a coach whose knowledge and experience can help hone their talent and keep them on the right path."

"What you're saying," mused Sarah, "is that the coach can make the difference between success and failure...or at least, between running for a local team and running in the Olympics."

"Exactly," Joe said. "And the more difficult the field, the more we need a coach. With society becoming more and more complex, we will need the help of more specialists and more experts than ever before. Therefore, the better qualified you are in your profession, the more of an expert you are, the more people will seek you out for advice. They will realize that it's much more productive to hire you than to try to do it themselves. That concept applies whether you're providing computer services or painting cars..."

"Or planning your finances!" Pete cut in.

> *"It's my job to tell my advisors where I want to go, and it's their job to tell me the best way to get there."*
>
> **—Neil Elmouchi**

"That's right!" Joe agreed. "I think that the most intelligent thing I've done over the years is to surround myself with the best coaches I could find. My attorney is my legal coach, my CPA is my accounting coach, and my financial planner is my investment coach. *My* talent is in running my business. I don't try to fool myself into thinking that I'm an expert like those professionals. I am much more comfortable drawing on *their* experience and *their* knowledge. It's my job to tell them where I want to go, and it's their job to tell me the best way to get there."

"And from where I sit," said Sarah, "this concept seems to be working pretty well for you."

"I think it is," Joe said as he glanced at his watch. "Gee, it's after four o'clock! I have to get going. Let's continue this discussion about the ten concepts over dinner one night next week?"

"Sounds great!" said Sarah.

"Name the date," Pete agreed.

> *"Nothing splendid has ever been achieved except by those who dared believe that something inside them was superior to circumstances."*
> —Bruce Barton

6

Understanding
Your Most
Valuable Asset

> *"Which sounds longer to you, 567,900 hours or 65 years? They are exactly the same. Regardless of our perceptions, time goes by whether we take action or not."*

On Tuesday evening, Pete and Sarah met with Joe for dinner at his country club.

"I thought this would be a good place to meet because we can take our time eating and when we are done we can head into the lounge and continue our discussion. It won't matter how late we want to stay," Joe assured Sarah and Pete.

Once they ordered dinner, Joe began to discuss concept number three. "Let's talk about your most valuable asset," he began.

"OK, what is it?" Pete inquired.

"What would you say it is?" Joe replied.

"I'd have to say my job," Pete answered. "Without it, I couldn't afford any of my other assets."

"What about you, Sarah?"

Sarah thought for a moment and then said, "My house. We've got a lot of equity built up there. It represents a majority of what Jim and I are worth."

Joe smiled. "Those are typical answers, and they're not bad ideas. But, neither one is your most valuable asset."

"So what is?" Pete challenged.

"Time." Joe stated matter of factly.

"Time?!" Pete and Sarah retorted, almost in unison.

"Yes. The foundation to all of your financial planning hinges on one basic ingredient: *time*. With enough time, you can turn even a small amount of money into enormous wealth."

"If you're lucky," Sarah declared.

"No, it's not just about luck. Luck can make you even wealthier, but time can do the job even if you're really cautious. Here, let me show you."

Joe launched into an example, the one his advisor had offered when they first started working together. "OK, Sarah, tell me, could you spare $2.00 a day if I told you I'd give you a million dollars in exchange for it?"

"Just $2.00 a day?" Sarah questioned.

"That's right." Joe confirmed.

"Of course I would," Sarah replied.

Joe smiled and started playing with his pocket calculator. "How about you, Pete?"

"In a New York minute."

"Hold on a second," chided Joe. "You've forgotten one very important issue. What are the conditions, what other ingredients am I going to add to this financial stew we're cooking up?"

"I don't know, but I bet you're going to tell us!" laughed Sarah.

"I sure am," Joe said as he took a piece of paper and a pen from his jacket pocket and placed it on the table. "Here are my assumptions. First, I'll give you that million dollars in exchange for your $2.00 daily payment, but I won't give it to you for forty-five years."

"Forty-five years?! I can't wait that long!" Pete protested.

Joe grinned and then continued: "My other assumption is that I can get an average rate of return of 12 percent on your money while I hold it for you."

"That's pretty optimistic, isn't it?" Sarah queried.

"Based on the performance of my portfolio over the years, I think it's a reasonable assumption. But, it's also why I wouldn't give the money to me if I were you," Joe smiled. "I'd give it to an *investment professional*. I'd have a lot more confidence in their ability to achieve a good overall return. They're experts in investing—I'm not.

"But, whatever the example," Joe continued, "I think the numbers speak for themselves. If you could give me $2.00 a day and earn an average of 12 percent a year for forty-five years, you would have a million dollars when we were through."

"That's pretty impressive, even if it does take a long time," Pete mused.

"Yes, it is," agreed Joe. "And think about what you just said, Pete. You said the magic word: *time*. Most people don't think about how important a factor time is when building wealth—at least, not until it's too late. Then, what do you hear them say? Something like, 'Gee, I should have started my savings years ago.' Not 'I should have put away more.' What they're saying is 'I wish I had more time.'"

> ## When you're out of time your out.

"I'm in that boat already," Sarah declared. "I can't wait forty-five years for my money to grow. I'm almost forty-five years old now, I'll be in a nursing home long before then!"

"Then you have to change the equation a little," Joe explained. "You have to start saving more money each year, to compensate for the time you've lost."

"How much more?!" Sarah challenged him.

"Well, now we're getting away from the concepts and into the details of a Strategic Life Plan. But I knew you would ask me this question so I brought along a copy of a quick reference chart you can take home. This chart can give you a better picture of how different amounts of money can grow at different interest rates over various periods of time."

(Refer to the chart at the end of this chapter)

"That will be interesting to look at." Sarah said as she took a copy from Joe.

"But I do have a couple of examples that can show you the relationship of time to money." Joe mentioned as he referred to his notes. "If you want your million in 35 years instead of 45, you'd have to invest about $6.35 a day. Or, if you want it in 25 years, then you've got to start with about $20.00 a day."

"Boy, it sure costs more the later you start, doesn't it?" Pete commented. "It's obviously easier to invest $2.00 a day than $20.00 a day!"

> *"I recommend to you to take care of the minute, for the hours will take care of themselves."*
> **—Lord Chesterfield**

"Exactly," said Joe. "That's why time is one of the most important investment concepts for you to understand. Time isn't just hours or days, it has a *value*. Every day that we're alive, we're spending time, whether we want to or not. That's why we have to look at money in the context of time."

"What do you mean?" Pete asked.

"The next time you're debating about whether to save an extra hundred dollars or to spend it on something you'd like, but *not* something you really need, don't fool yourself by saying, 'Hey, it's only a hundred dollars. What difference will it really make if I spend it or save it?' Add up all those '*it's just a hundred dollars'* statements over the months and years of your life, and it could make a huge difference. That's what I mean."

"What if I need to build that nest egg to a million dollars in 20 years, but I don't have all the extra money I need to invest?" protested Sarah. "I can't just pull the equity from my house and stop paying all my expenses to put that kind of money to work for me. We have to keep on living."

"That's precisely why you're putting together a financial plan," Joe replied. "Remember what I said earlier? I surround myself with experts and professionals and draw on their experience and knowledge. I tell them where I want to go, and they tell me the best way to get there. A good team of financial advisors can show you what you need to do, and help you predict how close you're likely to get to your ultimate goal, but *only* if you have a clear picture of where you are today and where you'd like to find yourself down the road."

"What if I find out that I just can't invest enough money to reach my goal?" Pete asked.

"Then you've got to rethink your goal, and make it more realistic," Joe replied. "If you can't reach 100 percent of your goal, maybe you can get to 90 percent or 80 percent. Don't be frustrated if you only reach 60 percent of your goal, consider where you would be if you did not do anything?"

"Up the creek without a paddle," Pete replied.

"Or a canoe," added Sarah.

"Yes," Pete agreed. "I'll be a lot better off doing something than doing nothing."

"That's the idea," Joe said. "No one can promise how much of your plan will be achieved over 10 or 20 years. But you can be sure that if you set up a plan and follow it, you will be much farther ahead than you would be without one."

"Makes sense to me," Sarah declared.

"Let's use our time wisely right now," Pete said with a smile as their dinner was being served, "and enjoy this wonderful meal."

How to Accumulate $1,000,000

**Regular Deposits Required to Accumulate $1,000,000
by Age 65 at Stated Rate of Return**

$ 1,000,000
12% Annual Interest Rate

Starting Age	Daily Savings	Monthly Savings	Yearly Savings
20	$ 2.00	$ 61	$ 730
25	$ 3.57	$ 109	$ 1,304
30	$ 6.35	$ 193	$ 2,317
35	$ 11.35	$ 345	$ 4,144
36	$ 12.77	$ 388	$ 4,660
37	$ 14.37	$ 437	$ 5,244
38	$ 16.18	$ 492	$ 5,904
39	$ 18.22	$ 554	$ 6,652
40	$ 20.55	$ 625	$ 7,500
41	$ 23.19	$ 705	$ 8,463
42	$ 26.19	$ 797	$ 9,560
43	$ 29.62	$ 901	$ 10,811
44	$ 33.52	$ 1,020	$ 12,240
45	$ 38.02	$ 1,157	$ 13,879
46	$ 43.19	$ 1,314	$ 15.763
47	$ 49.14	$ 1,495	$ 17,937
48	$ 56.05	$ 1,705	$ 20,457
49	$ 64.08	$ 1,949	$ 23,390
50	$ 73.49	$ 2,235	$ 26,824
51	$ 84.58	$ 2,573	$ 30,971
52	$ 97.75	$ 2,973	$ 35,677
53	$ 113.53	$ 3,453	$ 41,437
54	$ 132.64	$ 4,035	$ 48,415
55	$ 156.12	$ 4,749	$ 56,984

The figures shown above represent the amount of money you would have to save (i.e. daily, monthly, yearly), at the stated interest rate, in order to accumulate $1,000,000 by the time you reach age 65. These figures DO NOT take into account any federal or state taxes that may be incurred. Monthly and yearly figures are rounded to the nearest dollar.

How to Accumulate $1,000,000

**Regular Deposits Required to Accumulate $1,000,000
by Age 65 at Stated Rate of Return**

$ 1,000,000
10% Annual Interest Rate

Starting Age	Daily Savings	Monthly Savings	Yearly Savings
20	$ 3.81	$ 116	$ 1,391
25	$ 6.19	$ 188	$ 2,259
30	$ 10.11	$ 307	$ 3,690
35	$ 16.66	$ 507	$ 6,079
36	$ 18.49	$ 561	$ 6,728
37	$ 20.41	$ 621	$ 7,451
38	$ 22.62	$ 688	$ 8,258
39	$ 25.09	$ 763	$ 9,159
40	$ 27.86	$ 847	$ 10,168
41	$ 30.96	$ 942	$ 11,300
42	$ 34.44	$ 1,048	$ 12,572
43	$ 38.37	$ 1,167	$ 14,005
44	$ 42.81	$ 1,302	$ 15,624
45	$ 47.83	$ 1,455	$ 17,460
46	$ 53.55	$ 1,629	$ 19,547
47	$ 60.08	$ 1,828	$ 21,930
48	$ 67.57	$ 2,055	$ 24,664
49	$ 78.21	$ 2,381	$ 27,817
50	$ 86.23	$ 2,623	$ 31,474
51	$ 97.93	$ 2,979	$ 35,746
52	$ 111.72	$ 3,398	$ 40,779
53	$ 128.12	$ 3,897	$ 46,763
54	$ 147.84	$ 4,497	$ 53,963
55	$ 171.81	$ 5,229	$ 62,745

The figures shown above represent the amount of money you would have to save (i.e. daily, monthly, yearly), at the stated interest rate, in order to accumulate $1,000,000 by the time you reach age 65. These figures DO NOT take into account any federal or state taxes that may be incurred. Monthly and yearly figures are rounded to the nearest dollar.

7

The Difference between Wants and Likes

> *"Wanting **requires a commitment** – liking *only* requires an imagination."*
> —Neil Elmouchi

The three friends enjoyed their meal, talking about their work and families as they dined. When their coffee came, Sarah steered the conversation back to business: "You said something the other day about 'likes versus wants.' What did you mean by that?"

"That's concept number four on the list," Joe replied. "It focuses on the differences between really wanting something, feeling a sense of commitment toward achieving that goal, versus just saying, 'I'd like to have that.' *Wanting* requires a commitment – *liking* only requires an imagination."

"So what does this have to do with our financial plans?" asked Pete.

"Well, you can use this concept to help you target important goals and make important decisions in your life. It's not about what you want or would like for dessert, although that chocolate cake looks pretty darn good right now!" Joe laughed as his eyes glanced towards the dessert cart. "It's about what you want in the future, for yourself and your family. We're talking about really important issues, not something we choose to do impulsively, but things that will have meaning and value to you once you've decided to go after them."

"Like paying for your children's college education," mused Sarah.

"That's one of the biggies," Joe agreed. "Many people say they would *like* their children to go to college. But I figured out a long time ago that I wanted my kids to go. The difference between liking the idea and wanting to see it happen is that I started to plan for it. Laura and I kept on top of their schooling. We made sure they did their homework, encouraged them to do their best, and we met with their teachers when one of them was having a problem.

"We also laid the financial groundwork. We started a

college fund for each of them, to help cover tuition costs. This wasn't some passing fancy or just another dream that we hoped would magically come true. It was important to Laura and me, and we wanted it to happen. If there is any magic to the fact that one of our kids is in college and the other two are on their way, it's because we *wanted* to make it happen and committed ourselves to making it happen."

"But you've been making a substantial income for many years," Pete broke in. "What if you hadn't done so well?"

"I must tell you, Pete," Joe replied, "we started working on our children's college funds back when I was just getting my business off the ground. We didn't have much money and the bills came in faster than the income. Laura and I could have found plenty of little extras where we could spend our money, but instead, we put as much money into the college fund as we could. We were committed to achieving our 'want.' "

"So what you're saying," Pete declared, "is that 'wants' are what are really important, and 'likes' would be nice to have but they are not critical."

"That's right," Joe replied. "In my mind, a 'want' equals a commitment. If you *don't* feel strongly enough about a goal to commit to it, and you're not willing to do whatever you need to make it happen—then it is probably not a 'want.'"

"I'll bet I can name one of the most common 'wants,'"

challenged Sarah.

"I'll bet you can," smiled Joe.

"I think most people would like to be in a financial position to retire earlier than 65," declared Sarah. "I think it would be great to know that my investments would allow me to retire at 55 or even 50 if I wanted to. I may continue working, but it would sure be nice to work because *I want to* and not because *I have to*."

"Absolutely," said Joe.

"So if that's one of your *wants*," Joe continued, "you have to decide how much to put away to make it happen. The money you have to invest today in order to retire at 55 may mean that you can't buy a bigger house, or take as many vacations, or buy a new car every two years. The sacrifices may seem small to you, or they may seem big, but they will be worth making if you are truly committed to achieving that *want*."

"How do you decide if a goal is a *like* or a *want*?" Sarah asked.

"It's simple. Here's what my planner had me do. He told me to write down a list of all my dreams and desires—no matter how foolish they seemed—he wanted me to write them down. Then he told Laura to do the same thing. He told us not to do it all at once, to take a week or two, and jot down ideas as they came to us. When we were done, my list was four pages long, and Laura's was six!"

"Then, when we met with the planner the next time, he had us pretend that he was our own private genie, and he could grant us each twenty wishes. We had to go back to our lists and decide which twenty of our dreams were most important to each of us. It was really tough to do, but it was fun at the same time. We had to consider the pros and cons of each of our dreams. Doing that, we discovered that many of our fantasies weren't quite as important as we'd thought they were. When you have to choose, you start figuring out what really matters to you."

"Once we got our lists down to twenty wishes," Joe continued, "my planner played genie again and told us to cut our lists in half. Then when we got down to ten wishes each, he told us each to pick our five most important wishes. That was a real eye-opener! I had to decide what really mattered most to me, and I learned about Laura's hopes and dreams, too. We discovered that, while we shared some key dreams, we had some *wants* that were ours alone."

"Now it starts getting messy," joked Pete. "Did your advisor referee the fight?!"

"Well, I wouldn't describe what happened as a 'fight,'" Joe replied with a smile, "but I would say that we had a good, energetic discussion about what each of us considered our top priorities. The end result was worth it, because I think for the first time, we truly understood what each of us wanted out of life, and figured out which wants were important enough to both of us to build them into our Strategic Life Plan—and into our financial planning."

"It was just like we talked about the other day," Joe declared. "If you don't know where you are going, how will you know when you get there? This exercise clarified our important goals and put Laura and me on the same path. We identified the things we wanted to accomplish, which made it much easier to support each other when we had to make tough financial decisions."

"A wish list," Sarah said thoughtfully. "A list of everything I would like to have or accomplish in my life. No boundaries. No limits." She paused. "Sounds like fun!"

"It is," Joe agreed. "But don't rush it. Take your time and let your mind wander. Make sure Jim does the same thing," Joe said, looking at Sarah then shifting his eye to Pete. "And remember Pete, this is a fantasy list, so don't pass judgment on your wife's ideas. Your wishes aren't any more important than Marie's!"

"Is there any set number of wishes we should work towards?" Pete asked.

"Well, try to get at least fifty on your initial list. But it doesn't really matter, because the real work won't begin until you start to pare it down to twenty, and then ten and then five. When you each get down to five, put your list and Marie's together to get your top ten. Maybe it will be less than ten, if you have some of the same wishes. The list will give you plenty to start with in formulating your life plan."

"What happens when we accomplish something on the list?" Sarah inquired.

"Good question," said Joe. "Because that will happen. Over the years, you should be able to accomplish most of the things on your list. As you accomplish one wish, take it off the list and add the next most important item from your list of 20."

"And don't worry if one of your wishes 'falls off' the list. You may figure out a year from now, or five years from now, that something you considered really important today just doesn't matter as much to you anymore. Just drop it from your list and add something that does. After all, it's your life plan, you can do whatever you want with it!"

"Just be sure," Joe added, "to give careful thought to anything you add or delete. Your plan is a road map, so before you decide to take a detour, you should consider how the detour will affect your ability to reach your final destination."

"Sounds like a real challenge," Sarah remarked.

"But it sounds like fun, too!" Pete added.

"Yes, it does!" Sarah agreed. "I'll be curious to see what Jim puts on his list. I can already think of some items for my wish list.

"The more I learn about these concepts," Pete commented with enthusiasm, "the more anxious I am to start writing my own plan. Okay, Joe, what's the next concept on the list?"

> *"The measure of success is not whether you have a tough problem to deal with, but whether it's the same problem you had last year."*
> **—John Foster Dulles**

8

Establishing the Long-Term Perspective

> *"The journey of a thousand miles begins with one step "*
>
> —Lao-tse

❝Next up," Joe replied, "is learning how to maintain a long-term perspective of your objectives."

"OK," said Pete. "Sounds like an interesting concept. Explain away!"

"Sure. Let me give you an example," Joe replied, leaning back in his chair and taking a sip of coffee. "Suppose you decide to take a two-month vacation and drive from Los

Angeles to New York and back. Now assume you and Marie took a year to plan the trip. You carefully selected the cities to see, researched the various points of interest and national parks you didn't want to miss. Everything was accounted for from A to Z."

"Sounds great!" Pete remarked. "We like taking our time when planning trips. Is that the point about long-term thinking?"

"Not exactly. Imagine that the big day comes and you head off on your trip. Everything is going fine until day number eight."

"What happens?" Sarah inquired with a smirk on her face. "Do they get sick of driving? I know, they sold the car and took a plane to the Big Apple."

"No," replied Joe with a smile. "They still like their plan. But they hadn't planned on running over a nail and blowing out a tire. The tire was so badly damaged that they had to replace it instead of being able to have it repaired. Should they cancel the trip, Sarah?"

"No, I doubt that a ruined tire would stop them," Sarah declared.

"That's right," Pete agreed. "Replace the tire and we're on our way."

"OK," Joe said. "Now, about three days later, you hear a funny squeaking noise. You get it checked out at the dealership in the next big city you drive into, and find out that your brakes are shot. Do you cancel the rest of the trip now?"

"No," replied Pete, "but I might start feeling pretty dumb about not having the car checked out before I left!"

"Yeah, what's wrong with you anyway?" teased Sarah. "But a brake job wouldn't be the end of it. Things happen, and you take care of them."

"All right," continued Joe. "Another week into the trip, you're driving along, Pete, and there's a terrible noise under the hood. Your car loses power and you drift to the side of the road. You get towed to another repair shop, and the mechanic tells you your timing belt has broken. It'll be three days and $1,500 to repair the damage. What do you do now?!"

"I'd be pretty upset," acknowledged Pete, "but since we've planned this trip for a year, I think we'd want to finish it. We might have to skip some of our stops along the way to make up for lost time, but I wouldn't want to abandon our plans entirely. We'd have to take this as a temporary setback, especially since this is such a big trip. Problems were bound to arise."

"Good for you," declared Joe. "You have spent a long time planning this trip and you knew where you wanted to go and what you wanted to do. You knew that problems might crop up along the way; you wished that they wouldn't, but you knew they could. And you recognized that, in taking a long trip, you have increased your chances of having problems."

"You might have to start altering your plans a bit by now, since you've lost several days," Joe went on. "But you didn't just fold under the pressure and say, 'Forget it. Let's just head home.'"

"Well, you can't always have everything turn out exactly as you want it," Pete said. "You never know what will happen along the way."

"That's the next concept in action," smiled Joe. "You have to maintain a long-term perspective. You have to assume that there will be times when you question your earlier decisions, especially investment decisions. If your investment portfolio drops in value, you might start thinking about selling everything and playing it safe with your money."

"Isn't that kind of a knee-jerk reaction?" Sarah asked.

"It sure could be," answered Joe. "There are two responses to any problem. One is the quick, *'don't-think-just-react'* emotional response. What I've discovered over the years is that this kind of response is usually over-protective and pretty shortsighted.

"Then there is what I consider the *'wise response'*. But it requires a few logical steps, so you have to slow down a little to make it work.

"First," Joe explained, "you have to remind yourself what your long-term objective is. Second, you've got to consider whether the current problem can be viewed as a logical, anticipated 'bump in the road,' or whether it is a serious setback that will have a significant long-term impact on your Strategic Life Plan.

"Third," Joe concluded, "you ought to call your financial advisor and talk it over, so you can get another opinion from someone who is not as emotionally involved as you are in the situation."

"Think first, act later," Sarah summed up.

"You've got it," Joe smiled. "What this three-step response gives you is *time*. Time to sift fact from emotion. Time to think. There were many times when I've wanted to shift my investments because I became nervous over economic reports I heard on television or read in a newspaper article. I reminded myself that an emotional reaction was probably not a good investment reaction. I followed the advice I just gave you. I thought about my long-term perspective. I considered the severity of the situation. I called my financial advisor who helped keep me on track by reminding me of the financial course we charted. Talking with him turn my impulsive emotional reaction into a more rational intelligent evaluation.

"A long-term perspective is easy to talk about during good times but can be rather nerve racking when the economy is taking a beating and your portfolio drops in value. There have been a few times when I was ready to panic and sell everything, but after thinking the situation through, I realized it was a better time to buy then to sell! Every investor, even a wise, seasoned investor, can be tempted to panic once in a while. Having someone to talk to at those times, someone who has your best interest in mind and knows your long-range goals, will keep you calm and help maintain your long-term perspective."

"OK, now that we are taking the long-term perspective, do I get to finish my vacation?" Pete wondered.

"You're on your way," replied Joe with a laugh. "Just remember that it can take a great deal of emotional strength to stay on the highway when you seem to be running into one detour after another. That is when you must evaluate whether your fears are based on an emotional response or on valid concerns."

"And if they're valid?" quizzed Sarah.

"You make some adjustments," Joe replied. "But you stay on the highway."

"Speaking of highways, it's getting pretty late," Pete said. "I think I'd better hit the road."

"OK," Joe said. "How about finishing this up over dinner next Tuesday? I think you will find the last few concepts even more interesting."

"Sounds great," Pete declared. "You pick the place and I'll buy dinner."

"Sounds good to me, too," agreed Sarah. "What time should we be there?"

> *"Planning ahead is a measure of class. The rich and even the middle class plan for future generations but the poor can plan ahead only a few weeks or days."*

> *"No news is as good, or as bad, as it seems the first time you hear it."*

9

Never Gamble with Your Future

Gambling vs. Insurance "Gambling is creating a risk where none previously existed—insurance is protecting you against a risk that already exists."
—Neil Elmouchi

On Tuesday, Joe, Sarah and Pete met at Tuscany's, an Italian restaurant with great ambiance, excellent food and a quiet atmosphere which was ideal for continuing their discussion.

After placing their orders with the waiter and starting their dinner with a glass of wine, the discussion quickly reverted back to the remaining concepts.

Sarah started the discussion with a personal observation: "Joe, after last week's discussion, Jim and I spent time talking about each of the concepts. He found them equally intriguing. Interestingly enough, I found that these concepts made even more sense to me as I related your examples and stories to my husband. Now I am even more motivated to hear the rest of the concepts and apply them to my financial plan."

"I agree," said Pete. "I had some long talks with Marie about what we discussed and the need to put together a financial plan. In fact, she was very enthusiastic about each of us starting our *want's* list. Marie confided in me that she felt we should have been doing something like this for a long time but she didn't know where to start. I guess I've been too busy earning a living and not taking enough time to think about my family's financial security."

"I am glad to see that our talks are motivating both of you to start taking control of your financial futures," Joe said with a smile. "If you don't take charge of your life, who will?"

"That is exactly why I am anxious to hear the rest of the concepts!" Sarah said enthusiastically. "According to your advisor, the next concept title is 'Never Gamble with Your Future.' How does it tie in with financial planning?"

"It's really pretty simple," replied Joe. "I learned a long time ago that it just doesn't pay to take big risks when I don't have to. When I started putting together my financial strategy, I was fairly sure that I could get where I wanted to go. I knew it would take a lot of work and I never expected it to be easy, but I knew I could stick to the plan. I felt that as long as I was in control of my situation, I could create my own destiny.

"But, there was just one factor I knew I couldn't control." Joe continued.

"What was that?" Pete asked.

"My health."

"Why are you concerned about your health?" Sarah challenged. "You watch your weight and you exercise. You seem to be doing a pretty good job of it."

"I can watch my health," replied Joe. "But I can't control it. I learned that there are three major events that I can't control, and each one could make it difficult or impossible to reach my financial goals."

"What are they?" asked Pete.

"Well, the most obvious one is that I could die," replied Joe. "It could be a car accident or a heart attack or a terminal illness, you get the picture. In reality, death is part of one's financial planning. I know I can't avoid death. But, I can manage how it will affect my financial strategy.

"Second, I could become disabled. I don't know about you, but I know several people who have been disabled; one because of an accident and one because of a stroke. What happened to them could just as easily happen to me.

"Third," Joe continued, "I could get sick or be injured in an accident."

"How is that different from being disabled?" Sarah asked.

"Maybe I'd have a serious illness that didn't last too long, not enough to qualify as a long-term disability, but long enough and serious enough to rack up some big medical bills. Or it could happen to Laura or one of the children. Medical bills like that could literally wipe us out."

"But isn't medical insurance part of your financial plan?" Pete inquired.

"Of course it is," Joe replied. "But I'll tell you, the coverage I have now is a lot different from the coverage I bought when I put together my original plan."

"How?" Pete and Sarah asked.

"Well, what I'd thought was pretty good medical coverage didn't look so good when my advisor and I took a closer look at it. He helped me identify a number of big gaps in the coverage that I never knew existed. Under my old coverage, if I became seriously ill, I would have to personally pay out thousands of dollars for what the insurance didn't cover. Just because you have coverage doesn't mean that you've got the *right* coverage."

"But doesn't it get too expensive to cover everything?" Sarah protested. "It seems like all we ever do is pay higher insurance premiums."

"I know what you mean, Sarah," Pete agreed. "It seems like insurance companies are gambling that you're not going to need them, and you're gambling that you will need them."

"I can remember thinking that way," Joe mused. "At least until I read an article that opened my eyes about the difference between taking a gamble and protecting a risk. The article defined 'gambling' this way. It said: 'Gambling is creating a risk where none previously existed.'"

"Well, isn't risk what insurance companies are all about?" Pete demanded.

"You could say that," Joe replied. "But they're not creating a risk, they're protecting you from the risk. Consider this example: When I go to Las Vegas, I haven't gambled any of my money until I plunk down a hundred dollars on the blackjack table. I have no risk of losing the money in my pocket until I decide to place a bet. But, the moment I do, I create a risk. However, when I think about dying, becoming disabled or getting sick, I'm not creating the risk, that risk already exists."

"OK," agreed Sarah, "I understand what you are telling

us. Placing a bet in Las Vegas is my choice. It is a risk I can take, or avoid, the other risks are beyond my control."

"Precisely," said Joe. "When I started thinking about risk this way, I realized that I didn't want to take the responsibility of dealing with those risks alone. I may not be able to prevent an accident or an illness. I may not be able to avoid becoming disabled. But I can protect myself against the financial disaster that could follow. As for death, I know I'll die someday. I want to provide financial protection against this risk too.

"I don't like paying insurance premiums any more than the next guy, but I really don't like gambling with my whole financial future when I can transfer the financial risk to someone else. In other words, why take on the whole risk when it is more cost effective to pay an insurance company to protect me?"

"So," Pete declared, "I see your point. I'm really not gambling when I buy insurance."

"That's right," answered Joe. "The truth is, you're gambling if you *don't* buy the insurance."

"Paying them to take the risk for me can get pretty expensive," Pete argued. "Sometimes, it seems like we're spending so much on premiums that we're insurance-poor."

"Maybe it's less a matter of being insurance-poor, than a

matter of having poor insurance," Joe replied. "You shouldn't try to fool yourself into thinking it's okay to protect your family with a modest amount of insurance in order to save a few dollars on the premiums. Personally, I think the risk is too great. But it's all a matter of balance."

"The first thing you have to do when you're buying insurance," Joe continued, "is really understand your risks. And my risks are bound to be different than yours."

> *You don't get as much insurance as you can, you get as much insurance as you need.*

"What do you mean?" Sarah asked.

"Well, as an example, my kids are nearly grown, and we've already put aside the funds for their college costs. So the need for insurance to protect my children's education is behind us. But for you and Pete, it's still likely to be part of your financial plan. If either one of you were to get sick or become disabled or die, you would want to know that you provided a source of funds for their education.

"By the same token," Joe continued, "as that need disappears, other ones come into play. If I were to die today, the amount of money Laura would need is actually more now than it was a few years ago. However, because my portfolio has grown, the amount of insurance needed is reduced, since more income can come from the investments we've accumulated and less will need to be supplemented by insurance."

"Sounds like a pretty complicated balancing act," said Pete.

"It's really not that difficult," Joe continued. Even though the process can sound complicated, the idea behind it is pretty simple: *Risks do exist*. The biggest gamble you can take is *not* to protect yourself against those risks."

"So, you need to get as much insurance as you can?" asked Sarah.

> *It's just as important to have the right kinds of insurance as it is to have the right amount of insurance.*

"Not exactly," Joe replied. "It's important not to get a distorted view of what you should and should not do. You don't get as much insurance *as you can*, you get as much insurance as you *need*. It's just as important to have the right *kinds* of insurance as it is to have the right *amount* of insurance."

"Give me an example," Pete asked.

"Sure. If you heard that a good friend of yours had just

died and left behind a wife and two kids, what would be one of the first questions to run through your mind?"

"How much life insurance did he have?" replied Pete.

"Okay, and Sarah, if you heard that a co-worker had a freak accident when he was skiing and had been paralyzed for life, what would you wonder about first?"

"How much disability coverage did he have?" Sarah answered.

"Exactly right," said Joe. "Notice that each of you talked about a different kind of coverage. Our security is directly tied to the availability of money. It may not make us happy, but it sure will prevent a great deal of pain and suffering if the money is there when we need it. If the first person had a substantial amount of disability coverage and a puny life insurance policy, his family would be in trouble. If the second person had adequate life insurance but no disability insurance, his financial security would have disappeared. The point is simple—you not only need to have enough insurance—but you also need to have the right types of insurance."

"How did you figure out how much was enough for you and Laura?" Sarah asked.

"And what kinds of insurance did you buy?" added Pete.

"Actually, I didn't figure out how much or what types of coverage I needed. At least, not by myself," Joe replied. "I worked up a plan with my advisor that identified what I wanted to do for my family and how much it would take at that time to do it. Then we looked at some insurance programs—from inexpensive plans to ones with all the bells and whistles—and talked about the pros and cons of each one.

"It took a while," he added, "but ultimately we found a combination of programs that fit my budget and did the job we wanted them to do. If you take your time and think it through, you can put together a total risk management package that works. And if you don't, you're risking your financial security."

"Sounds like a very logical approach to solving the insurance problem," Pete said. "I'd like to find out if I'm spending my insurance money wisely. Maybe I can reduce my premiums."

"It is a good time to check it out," smiled Joe. "Because the only time you can get the insurance you really want is when you don't need it. Remember, it is your *health* that allows you to buy it, your *money* only pays for it."

> *It is your health that allows you to buy insurance, your money only pays for it.*

10

The Only Guarantee
in Life
is that Everything
Involves Risk

> *"Let your emotions rule your investment decisions, and you will destroy all your careful planning."*
>
> — Neil Elmouchi

Sarah's face lit up and she commented, "I'm starting to see a pattern here, Joe! All of these concepts *seem* to center on the idea that you must keep your eye on what is important to you, whether it is making the most of the time you have available to build a nest egg, or buying the right kinds of insurance to protect the nest egg."

"That's right," agreed Joe. "Each of these concepts helps you focus on what is important, and they make you realize that many beliefs you thought were important were really just clutter, obstacles in the way of achieving your own financial and personal security."

"So what are we getting at with the next concept?" Pete asked. "A minute ago, you were telling us not to create risk. Now you're telling us everything we do will involve some kind of risk! As far as investments are concerned, I tend to play it safe with savings accounts or insured CDs. You know, things that are guaranteed. Where's the risk in that kind of thinking?"

"Well, Pete, the only thing I can tell you is what my father always told me: 'There's only one guarantee in life, that every choice you make carries with it a certain amount of risk.' "

"Well, sure, if you go for high-return investments," countered Pete. "Like the example you gave us the other day, where we were getting a 12 percent return. I've always been told that the higher the return, the higher the risk. So what's the risk if I keep my investments in guaranteed products?"

"What we're talking about is not the investment risk, but rather your own *personal risk comfort zone*." Joe explained. "Every decision carries some risk. You might risk losing your funds by investing in a really speculative investment, or you might risk losing out on a really good investment opportunity by playing it too safe. Either way, you've said something about your tolerance for risk.

"It's important that you balance your 'risk tolerance' with your investment strategy," Joe went on. "Every wise investor knows that investing takes planning and patience. They also know that it involves risk. And they know that the kiss of death for any financial plan is emotion, especially when that emotion is greed or fear.

"Let your emotions rule your decisions, and you will destroy all your careful planning." Joe warned.

"So how do you keep emotions out of the equation?" Sarah asked.

"The best way," answered Joe, "is to design a portfolio that minimizes the possibility of you leaving your *risk comfort zone*. If you start panicking when you review your investments, you've left the *zone*. When you do that...when you start worrying that you are going to lose it all, you are probably going to lose sight of your long-term goals. This is when you are likely to call your broker or financial advisor, and scream, 'Sell everything before I've got nothing left!' Do that and you've undone all of your hard work."

"But what if things really are looking bad?" Sarah questioned.

"There is an old investor's adage," Joe replied, "that says, 'Buy on bad news and sell on good news.' If you really think about it, it makes sense. For most people, this is really hard to follow, especially when you are continually bombarded in the newspaper and TV about how poor the economy is performing or how bleak the economic future may be looking.

"Many times, making appropriate investment decisions is a matter of being well informed about your choices," Joe continued. "Being better informed may also increase your risk comfort level. So, even though your portfolio should not have a *collective risk level* greater than you're willing to accept, it may contain some investments that have a higher risk than others. A small amount of higher risk investments may help to balance your portfolio and increase its potential for a better overall return. However, you should not increase the number of higher risk investments in your portfolio until you have determined the level of risk you can tolerate."

"How do I determine my risk tolerance level?" Pete asked.

"In a technical sense," Joe answered, "it's the amount of portfolio volatility, or the amount of fluctuation in your investment value you can live with before you get too nervous and feel like you should be cashing out that investment. It's the point at which your ability to make a rational investment decision is overtaken by emotion, and you stop paying attention to your plan or listening to your financial advisor.

"Now that point is going to be different for each of us," he went on. "Only you know how much value your portfolio can lose in a down market before you start to panic. Only you know how comfortable you can be with the idea that equity investments aren't guaranteed, and that their value will fluctuate over time."

"It's easy to take more risk when the stock market is going up," remarked Sarah.

"Sure!" agreed Joe. "Nobody complains then. But when the market is dropping, and your portfolio loses 10 percent of its value, only you know if you can look at the situation as a great opportunity to buy stocks and mutual funds at distressed prices or if the situation will only make you very nervous."

"So how do you decide what's right for you? How do you become better informed to make the right decisions?" Sarah asked.

Joe looked at Sarah and started to direct her thinking. "Begin by asking yourself some questions. How would you react, for example, if your investments lost 10 percent of their value over the next year? How about 20 percent? Would you hold them for the long term or sell them? What if you had a 30 percent loss? Or 40 percent? At what point will fear set in for you? Your limit will be different from Pete's or mine. But you've got to figure out what your fear point is so you can use it to structure a portfolio that is sufficiently diversified to help you avoid reaching that point.

"This is one area where a good financial planner can be worth his or her weight in gold. A professional advisor can help you clarify your *investment comfort zone* and then assist in designing a portfolio that has a level of risk you can live with or at least tolerate.

"If you stay above your fear point," Joe continued, "you will be able to maintain your composure. You will continue to be a wise investor. If you reach your fear point, you will be on the phone, yelling and screaming at your financial advisor. That is a point you never want to reach."

"The whole thing seems like a roller coaster ride to me," Pete complained.

"Well, in a way it is," Joe said. "Investing in a portfolio for which the sole purpose is to get a maximum return, without recognizing the fact that you will have some ups and downs along the way, is an investment disaster waiting to happen. You must decide just how exciting a roller coaster ride you are willing to take, before you get on the ride.

"Years ago," Joe added, "I was pretty conservative. I worked hard for my money and I sure did not want to lose it.

However, as time went on, I learned more about how the market worked. I learned not to panic when my portfolio value dropped a bit. It's all a matter of keeping a long-term perspective, so I can ride out the storms along the way. When I made my investment choices, I accepted the level of risk with which I could maintain a calm and rational attitude.

"That is why it's so important to work with someone who knows you and knows how much risk you are willing to tolerate," Joe said. "A good financial planner will listen to you and design a portfolio that stays within your comfort zone. With professional advice, you can make informed decisions. Being informed can make all the difference in the world. It's empowering."

"I see the point of this concept, Joe," Sarah acknowledged. "I do want to get a good return on my investments, but Jim and I have not been risk takers in the past. Based on what you have said, I have a better appreciation of the need to balance our investment objectives with our risk tolerance."

"Yes," Pete interjected, "I agree with Sarah. I also have a better appreciation for using a financial advisor to help me find an appropriate mix of investments to fit Marie's and my comfort level."

"Well, I am pleased these concepts have been helpful in

making both of you appreciate the need to be wise investors, " said Joe with a smile, as the waiter brought the dessert tray. "Now, there's something I can *really* appreciate!"

If you don't take charge of your life, who will?

"You can be young without money, but you can't be old without it."
—Tennessee Williams

"Money is like a sixth sense without which you cannot make complete use of the other five."
—W. Somerset Maugham

11

Are You a Lender or an Investor?

> *"Put not your trust in money, but put your money in trust."*
>
> —Oliver Wendell Homes

J oe put down his dessert fork and remarked, "My financial advisor had another interesting point when he talked to me about risk and return. He told me I had two choices: *to loan my money or to invest it.*"

"Well, if you loan your money at a good rate, isn't it the same as an investment?" Pete asked.

"Not really. He said that whenever I make an investment that guarantees a particular return, I must look at the big picture. For example: Suppose I put $10,000 into a savings account, and the bank guarantees me 5 percent interest. Would you consider that to be a reasonable return in today's market?"

"It's a pretty good return these days," answered Sarah.

"And I would feel secure knowing I'm guaranteed that rate of return. There's no risk," Pete added.

"All of that is true," said Joe. "But there's one factor you ought to consider before you give the bank your money."

"What?" asked Pete.

"You must recognize that if the bank is giving you 5 percent, they're not earning just 5 percent on your money. They will earn more or they will lose money on the deal. They believe that if they are going to give you 5 percent for your money, they need to earn another 2 or 3 percent to cover their costs and make a profit.

"And that 3 percent is probably their minimum target return. If they're doing their job right, they're earning more. Maybe they're earning as much as 10 percent above your 5 percent. In effect, your 5 percent return is merely their cost of doing business. If they can loan your money out at 12 or 14 or 15 percent, then they're entitled to the difference."

"But I'm still getting what I wanted out of the deal," Pete replied. "So what's the problem?"

"There's nothing wrong with it," said Joe, "as long as it's the best investment you can make within your Risk Comfort Zone. Whether they make 1 percent or 100 percent isn't really relevant to you, as long as you decide that you want to be a lender. Accept this deal, and you have become a banker, lending your money to a banking institution which will, in turn, lend it to someone else. The positive benefit of this transaction is that you've guaranteed yourself a 5 percent return for the period of time you have lent them your money.

"But," Joe added, "that can also be a negative."

"Explain that," Sarah demanded.

"Well, you are sure to get 5 percent, but you are also sure that you won't get any more. By taking the position that you would like to loan your money because you are guaranteed a particular return, you are allowing someone else to make money on your money, because there is no way they will guarantee you a set return unless they are sure they can make even more money.

"Why would you do this?" challenged Joe. "Why not eliminate the middleman and invest your money instead of loaning it?"

"The risk is higher," Pete replied.

"Yes, that's true," acknowledged Joe. "When you invest your money, whether it's in stocks, mutual funds or another investment, you are accepting a certain level of risk. But you're also making it possible to enjoy the rewards if you invest wisely while the value of your investment goes up."

"How can you be sure one investment is better than a loan?" asked Sarah.

"There is no guaranteed way," responded Joe. "But you should start by understanding the differences between lending and investing. Knowing these differences will make you a more intelligent investor. It will help you decide for yourself which opportunity fits your needs.

Joe pulled some papers out of his coat pocket. "Let me show you a copy of a chart my advisor gave me. An independent service he uses tracks the performance of stocks, bonds, U.S. Treasury Bills and inflation. Looking at this information helped me to get a better understanding of the historical performance of these different investments. It also gave me a broader perspective regarding the rationale for diversifying investments so I have a better chance of getting the maximum return, given my level of acceptable risk."
*(Refer to charts at end of this chapter.)

"You should weigh each of your choices on the basis of three factors: First, how much *time* you have to allow each investment to work. Second, how will your investments *compliment* each other for a maximum overall investment return.

This is sometimes referred to as *diversification* or "asset allocation." Third, how much risk you are *willing to accept* to get the rate of return you want."

"So how do you get the *right* investment mix?" Sarah asked.

"There is no one right way," replied Joe. "The blend of investments that feels right to me will be different than the investment mix that is right for you. It gets back to the notion of concepts versus details. If I can identify my risk tolerance level, if I can clarify the concept, then I can turn to a professional to make the investment recommendations. He or she is the one who provides the details."

"By taking the safe route," Pete mused, "you are telling me that I will give up a larger potential return on my investment. I am giving up opportunities for security."

"That's right," Joe responded.

"But I might lose some of my money if I go the investment route," Sarah continued.

"Maybe," Joe said. "I am not an investment expert, but there is always the possibility that your portfolio will lose value during certain economic periods and increase in value at other times. However, that is not where I focus my attention. I am more concerned with the general direction my investments are moving rather than the short-term ups and downs. That is why you should diversify your investments, to minimize the downside risks and to help you keep a long-term perspective on your investments."

"What's your experience been?" asked Pete.

"My portfolio has had some very good years," Joe replied, "and it has had some pretty bad years. Overall, I have done considerably better than I would have if I had solely invested my money into a savings account or government bonds. In fact, there is no way I would be considering retirement in the next few years if I hadn't been willing to accept some risks as I built my portfolio.

"I always made sure that my portfolio had some equity investments, like stocks and mutual funds; and that it also had other types of investments, like bonds. I also had a small amount of my portfolio in cash or money market accounts in order to keep a portion of my funds liquid. The combination of the various investments gave me the overall return I wanted without going beyond my risk comfort level."

"So should I be taking more risks?" Pete inquired.

"How much risk you are willing to take is always a *personal* decision," Joe replied. "What I am suggesting is that your overall portfolio should be as aggressive as you can comfortably tolerate. That is much different than deciding to play it safe."

"How is it different?" Sarah cut in.

"To most people," Joe answered, "playing it safe means putting your money in some sort of guaranteed account: a savings account, CD, or government security. They usually offer a fairly low interest rate, but there is little or no risk of losing money."

"Howeer, by taking just a bit more risk, you might increase your return by several percentage points. Over time, 2 or 3 percent can make a big difference."

"Well, when you put it that way, with a chance of a better return, I would probably take a little more risk," said Pete.

"I thought you would," Joe smiled. "If you understand a particular investment's level of risk, you can decide if it falls within your comfort level.

"It has always been my philosophy to invest to the maximum boundaries of my risk comfort level. I have realized over the years, as I invested more and became more knowledgeable, I was willing to expand my level of risk tolerance."

"If I understand you correctly," Sarah commented, "the essence of this concept is to make sure you don't get swayed by investment stories about doubling your money in two years or some other get-rich-quick investment without making sure you are comfortable with the accompaning risk."

"Don't merely consider how much profit you might make and ignore the related risk, or it could come back to haunt you." added Pete.

"Very good! I think you've got it!" Joe smiled again.

Value of a $10,000 Investment At the End of Each Time Period

INDEXES	5-year 7/91 to 6/96	10-year 7/86 to 6/96	15-year 7/81 to 6/96
S & P 500	$ 20,743	$ 36,478	$ 88,025
LB Long Term Treasury	$ 16,465	$ 23,790	$ 63,717
LB Aggregate	$ 14,871	$ 22,714	$ 53,096
3 Month CD	$ 12,470	$ 17,974	$ 29,178
CPI (Consumer Price Index)	$ 11,514	$ 14,299	$ 17,286

Annualized Return Percentage

INDEXES	5-year 7/91 to 6/96	10-year 7/86 to 6/96	15-year 7/81 to 6/96
S & P 500	15.71%	13.82%	15.60%
LB Long-Term Treasury	10.49%	8.92%	13.14%
LB Aggregate	8.26%	8.55%	11.77%
3 Month CD	4.51%	6.04%	7.40%
CPI	2.66%	3.64%	3.72%

Refer to Glossary for definitions of indexes listed above.

Past performance of any investment, indexes or class of assets is never a guarantee of future performace.

Source: Principia for Mutual Funds, Morningstar, Inc., Chicago, IL — 312-424-4288

Value of a $10,000 Investment at the End of Each Time Period

Mutual Funds	5-year 7/91 to 6/96	10-year 7/86 to 5/96	15-year 7/81 to 6/96
Pacific Stocks	$ 16,006	$ 33,223	$ 78,294
Small Company	$ 24,057	$ 34,723	$ 76,873
Growth	$ 20,260	$ 32,139	$ 73,609
Aggressive Growth	$ 24,690	$ 36,165	$ 73,344
Growth & Income	$ 19,375	$ 29,832	$ 68,303
World Stock	$ 18,599	$ 28,890	$ 64,427
Balanced	$ 17,317	$ 26,344	$ 62,812
Foreign	$ 16,276	$ 26,346	$ 61,239
World Bond	$ 15,416	$ 23,971	$ 51,268
Corporate Bonds - General	$ 14,569	$ 21,128	$ 47,000
Government Bonds - Treasury	$ 14,531	$ 20,851	$ 46,732
Government Bonds - General	$ 13,758	$ 19,709	$ 38,965
Municipal Bonds - National	$ 13,970	$ 20,067	$ 37,674
Diversified Emerging Markets	$ 17,991	$ 24,962	$ 36,459
CPI (Consumer Price Index)	$ 11,514	$ 14,299	$ 17,286

Above mutual fund classes are listed in descending order based on their 15-year performance. Please note that different classes of mutual funds DO NOT always out perform other fund classes during every time period. The top three performing mutual fund classes for each time period are highlighted in bold ink..

Past performance of any investment, indexes or class of assets is never a guarantee of future performace.

Source: Principia for Mutual Funds, Morningstar, Inc., Chicago, IL — 312-424-4288

Annualized Return Average

Mutual Funds	5-year 7/91 to 6/96	10-year 7/86 to 5/96	15-year 7/81 to 6/96
Pacific Stocks	9.86%	12.76%	**14.70%**
Small Company	19.19%	13.26%	**14.56%**
Growth	15.17%	12.38%	**14.23%**
Aggressive Growth	19.81%	13.72%	14.21%
Growth & Income	14.14%	11.55%	13.67%
World Stock	13.21%	11.19%	12.22%
Balanced	11.61%	10.17%	13.03%
Foreign	10.23%	10.17%	12.84%
World Bond	9.04%	9.14%	11.51%
Corporate Bonds - General	7.82%	7.77%	10.87%
Government Bonds - Treasury	7.76%	7.63%	10.83%
Government Bonds - General	6.59%	7.02%	9.49%
Municipal Bonds - National	6.92%	7.21%	9.25%
Diversified Emerging Markets	12.46%	9.58%	9.01%
CPI (Consumer Price Index)	2.86%	3.64%	3.72%

Above mutual fund classes are listed in descending order based on their 15-year performance. Please note that different classes of mutual funds DO NOT always out perform other fund classes during every time period. The top three performing mutual fund classes for each time period are highlighted in bold ink.

Past performance of any investment, indexes or class of assets is never a guarantee of future performace.

Source: Principia for Mutual Funds, Morningstar, Inc., Chicago, IL — 312-424-4288

12

Know the Rules *before* You Play the Game

> *If you ignore the rules, the government will assume that you would rather give them your hard earned money, instead of to your spouse, children or other heirs.*

"The next concept caught my eye," declared Sarah. "If planning your financial strategy is so important, why are we talking about playing games?"

"What game are you referring to?" inquired Pete.

"The best way I know to describe this concept," replied Joe with a smile, "is to talk about a game we played as kids."

"Which one?" Sarah asked.

"Monopoly."

"That sounds good," said Pete. "The game involves money, property, risk...all the concepts we have been talking about."

"Right. But there are a few assumptions you must agree to before we play this version of the game," said Joe.

"Such as?" asked Sarah.

"First, you have to play as though neither of you has ever seen the game before. You are not familiar with its strategies. We simply open up the game board and put the pieces on the table. Then we play."

"Sounds fair enough," Sarah responded.

"Okay," grinned Joe. "So what's the first thing you'll want to do?

"Learn the rules," replied Pete.

"Exactly. Otherwise, how could you play? So, being the nice guy that I am, I will tell you the rules you need to know to get started: You roll the dice, move your tokens, and start buying property. It all seems pretty straightforward, doesn't it?"

"Yes it does," said Pete. Sarah nodded her head in agreement.

"Well it is pretty simple...in the beginning. We play for a while and both of you do pretty well. In fact, you both acquire several pieces of property and put away some cash."

"I wish I was doing that well in real life!" joked Sarah. "Sounds like we are doing fine. So where's the problem?"

"Well, Pete's next move starts to change his good fortune," Joe replied.

"And what dumb thing did I do?" laughed Pete.

"You land on one of my properties," explained Joe. "And it's my most valuable property. So you owe me a large amount of money."

"Sorry, Pete," Sarah teased. "And you were doing so well."

"I wouldn't get too smug if I were you, Sarah," cautioned Joe.

"Okay. What's my problem?!"

"You start having your own run of bad luck," Joe replied.

"How did that happen?"

"Remember how I told you just enough rules to get you started?"

"Yes."

"Well," replied Joe, "you should have learned more. You

were willing to start playing the game, without learning all the rules. Since I was aware of those rules, I took advantage of them as I played the game."

"That's not really fair," protested Pete. "Why should we be subject to rules we didn't know existed?"

"Keep that thought," Joe said with a smile. "If you follow this imaginary Monopoly game further, you will discover that by not knowing the rules, the property and money you accumulated in the beginning of the game is now being lost by one bad move after another. In fact, you're losing most of what you accumulated."

"So what you are telling me, Joe," interrupted Sarah, "is that when we started to play this game we understood enough of the rules to get started. But because we didn't understand all the rules, certain unforeseen obstacles are now causing us to lose what we accumulated."

"Very good," replied Joe. "You're starting to get the concept. Now, let's change the name of the game from 'Monopoly' to 'The Game of Life.' Imagine yourself as one of the pieces on the game board. As you move through life, you are confronted with the rules and laws of society and government. Some of the rules you were taught as a child, simple rules like respecting other people's property, not running red lights, looking both ways before you cross the street. Others you learn as you get older, which determine how we operate, how we work with other people, how we interact as individuals with the government."

"Well, this is all pretty interesting," interrupted Sarah, "but what does it have to do with putting together a financial strategy?"

"Everything," replied Joe. "You must learn and understand *all* the rules if you expect to come out a winner. Let me give you a more concrete example."

"Good, I'm still a little confused," commented Pete.

"Okay," said Joe. "A few years ago, a good friend of mine was killed in an auto accident. Ben was forty-six, and he left behind a wife and two kids. He had been a very successful real estate developer, and he was like a brother to me."

"A few weeks after the funeral, Ben's wife, Linda, called and asked me to serve as executor of his estate. Of course, I agreed. I started to work with Ben's attorney and accountant a few days later, to be sure all of his property was transferred according to his wishes. Let me tell you, this experience really opened my eyes."

"In what way?" asked Sarah.

"I realized that there were many rules to the financial strategy game that I had not paid attention to. These rules related to proper preparation of one's estate."

"Like what?" inquired Pete.

"Even though Ben was very wealthy, he was always focused on accumulating wealth. He never took time to learn about the rest of the rules. The rules that dealt with retaining your wealth. His death could not have happened at a worse time. It was going to cost his family a bundle of money and a great deal of emotional turmoil."

"Sounds like a mess," Sarah commented.

"It was. It was a very big mess."

"What were the problems?"

> *"You think you understand the situation, but what you don't understand is that the situation just changed"*
> **—Putnam Investment Advertisement**

"First, he had a will, but it was outdated," Joe explained, "When he wrote it, he left some money to his parents, but they passed away after the will was written and he never changed it.

"Second, different properties were titled in different ways. Some were held jointly with Linda, some were owned by Ben himself, and some he owned with his partners. There were no business agreements regarding how the property was to be sold to his partners.

"Third, Ben owned all of his life insurance and it was to be paid directly to his estate. There was no trust to put the proceeds into. This resulted in most of Ben's property having to pass through probate. Since there were no buy-sell agreements for his business interests, an independent appraiser had to be hired to value it for tax purposes. There was no..."

"Wait a second!" Sarah interrupted. "You mean to tell me that with all of that wealth, Ben never figured out how it should be handled should he die?"

"That's exactly what I'm saying," answered Joe. "He always figured he would have plenty of time for that later. He was too busy trying to accumulate wealth to be concerned with preserving what he had already acquired."

"He didn't learn all the rules of the game," declared Pete.

"That's right. And by the time we were done with all of the attorneys, accountants and appraisers; plus the probate court fees and the IRS, a huge chunk of what Ben had accumulated was gone."

"Gone?" Sarah asked. "How?"

"Expenses. Taxes." replied Joe, "And in large part because he had invested in the wrong type of assets."

"What do you mean?" asked Pete.

"Much of his estate was made up of investments and property that were not very liquid. It was worth a substantial amount on paper, but it couldn't be sold easily. While Ben was alive, the lack of liquidity was not an issue, because they lived on his salary. But when he died, those investments were Linda's only source of income. She needed money, not property, to support her family. So we had to sell most of the assets to raise money for them to live on. In the process, we lost about 40 percent of the asset value, because we had to sell when the market was weak."

"You mean a major portion of the wealth he accumulated during his life was lost because he didn't plan for its distribution in the event of his death?" asked Sarah.

"That's right. If Ben had sought professional advice to review his will, revise his tax strategies and to protect his business, he could have avoided most of those expenses and provide more wealth to his family.

"The way I look at it," Joe went on, "you are playing a game with the government. If you ignore the rules, the government will assume that you would rather give them your hard-earned money, instead of giving it to your spouse, children or other heirs.

If you are willing to take the time to use the tax laws to

your benefit, you and your heirs will be able to keep much or all of the taxes and expenses that would have been paid. You can pay the *maximum* tax or pay the *minimum* tax; the choice is yours."

"Are you saying that if I do proper planning my heirs won't have to pay *any* taxes?" asked Sarah.

"Not exactly," Joe responded. "In some cases planning can eliminate taxes; in other situations it can merely reduce the tax. I am not a tax expert, but I have seen enough to know that proper planning would have left Linda and the children in a much better financial position.

> *"In preparing for battle, I have always found that plans are useless, but planning is indispensable.*
> —Dwight D. Eisenhower

"Let me see if I understand this concept," Sarah interrupted. "This concept is telling us that the big picture may be bigger than we thought. The other concepts were more concerned with our wants, our desires, our objectives. This concept is warning us not to ignore the *rules of the game*: the tax laws, wills and trusts, estate costs and government regulations. All of these things are important because they can directly affect our ability to accumulate wealth while we are alive and our family's ability to retain the wealth at our death.

They can all have a major impact on our financial security."

"Exactly!" cheered Joe. "You must *know the rules* if you are going to make sure that you and your family can *keep* what you worked so hard to earn."

"But how can we know *all* of the tax laws and *all* of the rules?" Pete inquired.

"You can't," replied Joe. "That's why you need people who specialize in these areas and understand the rules, like an attorney, an accountant and a financial advisor. Together, they can show you how to play a winning game."

"What if you don't have much money to work with?" Pete questioned. "I don't have much property or investments just yet. It seems rather involved when I have so little with which to start."

"That's a good point!" Joe responded enthusiastically. "When you are just getting started, the rules of the game are relatively few and fairly simple. It may involve setting up a will or a trust or how you title your home. So you won't get too involved with advisors in the beginning.

"But," he continued, "as you develop your financial plan and your assets start to grow, you should guard against complacency. You should protect yourself against the feeling that 'I've done okay on my own so far; therefore, I can do it all myself.' To maximize your Strategic Life Plan, you must constantly keep an eye on tax strategies in order to take advantage of the best investment opportunities each step of the way. You should be ready to make changes as you accumulate assets. The only way you can do that right is to work with a professional."

"That makes sense," Sarah agreed. "I think I'll call both my attorney and my accountant next week. I would like to tell them what I am about to do and get their opinion."

"That's the way to think about it," agreed Joe. "Now, let's get on to the final concept."

> *You can pay the maximum tax or pay the minimum tax, the choice is yours."*

> "*I have always thought that one man of tolerable abilities may work great changes, and accomplish great affairs among mankind, if he first forms a good plan, and cutting off all amusements or other employments that would divert his attention, make the execution of that same plan his sole study and business.*"
>
> **—Benjamin Franklin**

13

If I Tell You where it Hurts, do I Still Have to Pay You?

> *"Money is better then poverty, if only for financial reasons."*
>
> —Woody Allen

❝Joe, you keep telling us to hire an investment advisor," Pete said. "How can I afford to do that when I haven't accumulated much money in my plan just yet? I don't think I can afford to pay for that kind of advice right now. Wouldn't I be better off investing the money I'd spend on the advisor, instead of eating up that money on fees?"

"You're asking the wrong question," Joe replied.

"What do you mean?" Sarah retorted.

"What question should I be asking?" Pete chimed in.

"You should be asking two questions," Joe explained. "The first one is, 'What parts of my Strategic Life Plan can I do myself?' The second question is, 'Who should I hire to help me with the parts of my plan that I cannot do myself?' "

"So how do we figure that out?" Pete inquired.

"Let me try to explain it. I'll start by telling you a little story:

A man goes to see a doctor for the first time, and he says to the doctor, "Hey, Doc, would you please write me a prescription for an antibiotic?"

"Why do you think you need an antibiotic?" the doctor asks.

"Oh, I'm not sure," the man replies. "I've just been hearing some good things about antibiotics, so I figured it would be a good idea to take some."

"Are you sick?"

"No. But I figure an antibiotic should help to keep me healthy."

"Which antibiotic did you have in mind?" the doctor inquired, in amazement.

"Gee, I don't know. Just give me one of the well-known brands, you know, the really good stuff."

"Are you aware that different antibiotics fight different germs?"

"Really? That's a good point, Doc. Maybe I should take a few of them to cover all the possibilities. You know—diversify."

"Well, maybe I ought to examine you to determine if you really need any of these antibiotics, and to decide which ones would be best for you," the doctor suggested.

"Thanks for offering, Doc, but I've done a lot of reading about health and medicine lately, and I think I've got this game pretty well wired. I've decided that, if I stick to the well-known medicines by the big pharmaceutical houses, and take a variety to cover all my bases, I'll be in pretty good shape. I'll be healthy, and I'll save a ton of money on doctor's bills. No offense, but I don't think this medicine business is as complicated as you guys make it out to be."

"Okay, okay," laughed Sarah. "We get the point, Joe."

"Yeah, so what is it?" Joe challenged.

"We're back to the idea that information isn't knowledge," Sarah replied.

"Just because we know something about investments doesn't mean we know how to choose them or how to diversify our choices," Pete interjected.

"That's the idea," Joe smiled. "Our patient got information from a variety of sources, but he really wasn't qualified to act on it independently. He made the mistake of assuming that information gave him knowledge. What the information should have done was to make him a more intelligent patient, someone who was more aware and more capable of asking important, relevant questions. The information should have improved communication between him and his doctor. It should have helped give him a sense of confidence in his doctor, not give him the idea that he could *become* the doctor."

"Okay, Professor," cut in Sarah. "Your point is well taken. Now, what about the second question?"

"Well," said Joe, "the second question was about hiring someone to help you in the areas where you are not an expert."

"Joe, I would love to have a professional advisor, but I can only afford so much. Isn't it going to be very expensive to get the kind of investment advice you've been talking about?" Sarah questioned.

"Not necessarily," Joe continued. "Try looking at it this way: When you go to a restaurant for breakfast, and you get your check, do you give a tip?"

"Sure," replied Pete. "I usually make it 15 or 20 percent...you know, depending on how good the food was and if I liked the service."

"That's the way we all do it," said Joe. "And it's sort of amazing."

"What do you mean?" Sarah asked.

"Well, do you realize how much you're paying just to have someone bring you a dish with your food on it? They didn't cook the food, they don't wash the dishes, and when you get done eating, you may never see them again in your life. But you were willing to give them 15 or 20 percent of the value of your purchase just because they spent a couple of minutes talking to you and taking your order."

"But that's the way it is," Pete replied.

"And what impact will that person have in helping you attain your financial future?" Joe asked.

"None," Sarah answered.

"That's right. So why are you so willing to give your money away in one situation and so concerned about what it will cost in another situation?

"What you have to consider when thinking of hiring a financial advisor is not 'How much will it *cost*?' You have to ask yourself, 'What is the *value*?' How much is it worth to have an independent third party spend hours with you, listening to your dreams and aspirations, helping you clarify your goals, and designing a plan that will help make you and your family financially secure?

"If getting those things are important to you..." Joe went on, "...if working with someone who can help you make good financial decisions, be there for you when the market is shaky, and will work with you from year to year...if all of that is important to you then, paying that person for their services to help you achieve your financial goals should not be considered an expense. He or she should be valued as *part of the investment* in your future."

"In other words, if it's worth more to you than a plate of ham and eggs," Pete declared with a smile, "it's worth paying for."

"So, if I understand what you're saying," Sarah broke in, anxious to express her thoughts, "as wise investors, it's our job to understand these investment concepts and to understand how they relate to our personal objectives. It's important to understand the broad picture but to delegate the details to a professional. It all goes back to your example of changing the oil in your car, even though you know why it's important to do it regularly, it makes more sense to have a trained technician do the actual work."

"Very good Sarah, you've been listening!" Joe said with a big grin. "It's concept versus implementation. It's more cost effective, and a better use of my time to pay someone else to change the oil in my car than to try to do it myself. Besides, I trust my mechanic. I know that if my car needs some other repairs, he is likely to spot them and tell me what I should do before the car has big problems."

"I think I finally have a clear picture of this whole idea!" Pete said enthusiastically, wanting to have an opportunity to verify that he is on the right track. "It's the difference between collecting information and acquiring knowledge. None of us can know everything. We must *rely* on the expertise and experience of other people, if we are going to benefit from their knowledge. Use the information you acquire to help you become an *informed consumer*, but don't fool yourself into thinking that you have become an *overnight expert*."

"Very good, Pete! You understand that concept!" said Joe.

"Believe it or not, I am *not* trying to convince you to hire a professional financial advisor," Joe went on, "but I *am* suggesting that you consider interviewing a few of them. I think you owe it to yourself to find out how they can work with you and how they set their fees. You may decide that the advisor is not an expense but really an asset."

"So it's more important to go to an advisor in the beginning, rather than down the road," Pete mused.

"The best time to talk to someone is when you're getting started," Joe agreed, "not after you've put in five or ten years and blown many opportunities by making the wrong investment choices."

"Well, Joe, you're the expert," Sarah declared. "If it

worked for you, I should at least check it out."

"It's better than flying blind," Joe agreed.

"Point taken," Sarah declared. "Now that we have learned the ten concepts, I can't wait to start putting my financial plan together."

"Before you run off to start writing your plan," Joe said jokingly, "let's celebrate with a toast."

"I second that motion!" said Pete. They all raised their wine glasses to acknowledge the completion of the first step on their way to taking control of their financial future.

Pete and Sarah went directly home after dinner. They were both anxious to tell their spouses the rest of the concepts and start putting together their financial plans. They had both thought about doing this type of planning in the past but it never seemed to get beyond the talking stage. This time it was going to be different. This time they had a clearer picture of what steps to take next. This time they had the support of their family. This time they were going to be wise investors.

> *"Life is a journey, age marks the time, experience marks the distance."*
> **—Neil Elmouchi**

14

The Wrap-Up

> *"Information can tell us everything. It has all the answers. But they are answers to questions we have not asked, and which doubtless don't even arise."*
>
> —Jean Baudrillard

Don't let the simplicity of this book disguise the importance of applying its principles. They are essential and fundamental concepts that should not be overlooked when establishing your own investment strategy.

One of the most common mistakes people make is allowing their business or their employment to become their primary income source. This occurs because most often it is critical to their financial security. It becomes their primary asset. What people tend to ignore is that both businesses and employment have life cycles. And too often they fail to appreciate, that without proper planning, their primary asset can diminish in value over the years.

The ultimate objective is to build a portfolio capable of generating an annual income sufficient to meet your standard of living. You want to be in a position to make work an *option* instead of a *necessity*. That is financial independence!

Acquiring financial independence is like preparing for a journey: To start this journey you should review and evaluate your current position. Begin by categorizing the assets: personal property, real estate, business interests and insurance. Confirm how your property is titled. Look at the diversification of assets. Analyze your income tax and estate tax exposure. Finally, ask yourself if your current wealth creation strategies are appropriate for your financial situation.

By doing these things — by evaluating your current financial situation—you will be taking the important first step toward developing a proper financial plan. From this point, you will be able to consult with other advisors, such as your accountant, attorney or financial planner, and make whatever changes you both agree are necessary.

Four Reasons People Delay Starting Their Own Plan

1. Lack of Expertise

If you do not feel comfortable writing your own Strategic Life Plan, then start interviewing financial specialists and choose one who you believe can offer customized broad-based investment guidance specific to your needs.

2. Lack of Time

Time is a big stumbling block for many of us. In today's fast-paced lifestyles, taking care of your business or career, and participating in the activities of daily life, can consume all of the hours in a day. It could be that you just don't have the time to research, evaluate and monitor a serious financial program. It may be more practical and cost-effective to seek assistance from a financial advisor to help you establish and monitor your plan.

3. Procrastination

Procrastination is the No. 1 killer of time. It is not uncommon to hear someone say, "Gee, I meant to start investing my money a long time ago," and then learn that their cash is still sitting in the bank, earning 2 or 3 percent interest; waiting for them to make a decision. They are caught in a double bind: they feel they should be competent enough to make decisions for themselves, but they are held back by fear—of making the wrong decision. There is always another excuse to delay their decision until tomorrow. *They are continually commencing to begin.*

4. Lack of Accountability

Finally, you must commit your Strategic Life Plan to writing. Writing a plan *before* you begin investing your first dollar is essential to enhancing your financial success.

A written plan provides the foundation for accountability. Time has a way of altering the facts, so if you are going to be true to your goals, you must commit them to paper. If you do that, your plan will acquire the power to mold your future; it will unlock the financial rewards that previously were nothing more than a dream. A financial plan will be one of the most powerful tools in your arsenal, for it will allow you to take command of your financial destiny.

The wise investor knows that effective use of his or her time offers the greatest promise for the greatest return. The rewards are much greater if we each focus on what we know best, and hire others to focus on the things they know best. When we waste our time, we are spending our most valuable asset in exchange for nothing.

Don't let these reasons delay your taking action. We have all found ourselves in situations where our intentions were the best, but we didn't feel comfortable about making decisions. We lacked the time to study all of the available information necessary to come to a final decision. There was always something else that had to be done first, so we would put it off until tomorrow...but tomorrow never came.

No more excuses! No more "tomorrows!" Make your commitment *now*!

> *"There is nothing new in the world except the history you do not know."*
>
> —Harry S. Truman

Time is Your Most Valuable Asset —

Spend it Wisely.

15

Concept Summaries

The purpose of this chapter is to summarize the ten concepts introduced in this book. Use this chapter as a reference point when you want to remind yourself of the essence of each of the concepts.

This chapter can become very valuable by re-reading it on a regular basis as a means of refreshing the concepts in your mind so that they can be applied as needed to your Strategic Life Plan.

❖   ❖   ❖

Concept #1

Information is not Knowledge.

The purpose of this concept is to provide an awareness for distinguishing between *gathering information* and *acquiring knowledge*. Having information is important, but converting it to usable knowledge that can be applied effectively isn't always easy.

Acquiring information can help make you more effective in selecting products or using the services of other professionals. However, it doesn't necessarily make you a professional just because you have read some articles or books on a particular topic. Knowledge is the accumulation of information combined with practical experience that allows you to develop effective skills in the particular area of interest.

Information can make you a more effective consumer. But, you should always consider using the services of a professional if the product or service involves the need for extensive expertise. An example of this would be using an attorney when drafting a will and trust, or an accountant when filing complicated tax returns.

Remember, you are encouraged to obtain as much information as possible about ways of accomplishing your ultimate goals. The combination of being well informed and using experts when appropriate will greatly enhance your ability to achieve your ultimate objective.

Concept #2

Why Olympic Athletes Have Coaches

Being able to excel typically requires knowledge and expertise in a number of areas related to that talent or profession. In today's fast-paced society, gathering all that information requires the combined efforts of more than one person. It is a better use of your time and resources to seek out experts who can give you valuable guidance. By drawing upon their knowledge, these experts let you focus on developing your talents.

It doesn't matter whether you call the person a coach, an advisor, a mentor or any other name. What does matter is that you find someone you trust, have confidence in, and has the experience to assist you in accomplishing your goals. The purpose of this concept is to remind you that you need someone who can understand your objectives and who can act as a sounding board for your ideas.

A good coach can help guide you along your path and keep you focused on your goals. This person could be an excellent resource to keep you in touch with reality and stop you from fooling yourself along the way. Having a coach makes you accountable. Even though the accountability is ultimately for yourself, we tend to be much more productive when we have to answer to someone else.

Spreading your energies in too many directions will help you accomplish only one thing: mediocrity. The secret of this concept is to focus your energies on those things you excel at and to draw upon other people's talents to assist you as needed.

❖　　　❖　　　❖

Concept #3

Understanding Your Most Valuable Asset

This concept is so simple many people tend to ignore it. *Time* is your most valuable asset. Anything you do that is not an effective use of your time is costing you money and some of the enjoyment of your life.

From an investment standpoin, you can accumulate an enormous amount of money if given enough time. However, should you start later in life, do not be disheartened. Even though the time and money available may not be as much as you would have wished, remember that anything you *do today* will be significantly more than had you *done nothing*.

Procrastination is the Achilles' Heel of this concept. Don't tell yourself you can do it tomorrow because Tomorrows turn into weeks, months and years. If you have not established a financial plan that will guide you towards your financial security, *do it now*, not tomorrow. Once you start a program make sure you review and monitor it on a regular basis. Make sure your precious time does not slip away. Regular monitoring will help confirm that you are on the right course. The only way you will know if your time is well spent, is to compare your actual results against your financial planning goals.

One of the easiest ways to get started is to focus on the big picture. Focus on the goals and objectives you want to accomplish. Don't worry about the details; they are merely the steps along the path that get you to your ultimate destination. Too many people develop a mental block to this whole process by worrying about each little detail. They are consumed by the specifics to such an extent that they ultimately lose sight of the big picture. You can not expect to be competent in each aspect and detail necessary to accomplish your goals. Some of those details are better delegated to other people who have expertise, knowledge and experience in that aspect of your total plan.

Therefore, when looking at the details, consider the energy and time required to do it yourself. It could be more cost effective and faster to hire someone. Don't fool yourself into believing that just because you are doing it yourself you're saving money. The wise investor focuses on what he or she does best and delegates everything else.

Concept #4

The Difference between Wants and Likes.

We are continually being tempted by different material desires on a daily basis. Whether it is buying a new car, taking a vacation, or just purchasing new clothes. There is always something that tends to motivate us to spend our money. The only way to take control of your financial destiny is to know what is truly important to you and avoid being tempted by immediate emotional impulses.

Following the exercise described in this chapter will help you distinguish between *"wants"* and *"likes."* Be sure to make a list of at least 50 items or more that you believe you *want*. If you are married or have a significant other, have him/her write his/her own wish list. Each person should feel free to make their own list without fear of being criticized by their partner. The first list should contain all of your dreams and aspirations, no matter how wild or impossible they may seem at the time. Take your time! This list gives you the opportunity to fantasize. It's all right if it takes you a couple of weeks to complete this exercise. Just remember, it is important to go with your first thoughts and not try to filter or critique your list during the first draft.

After completing your initial list, each of you should decide which are the *20* most important items on your list. Once each wish list is pared down to 20 items, it is time to rethink the list and reduce it to the ten most important items. If each of you is developing your own list, you are each allowed to choose your 5 most significant *"wants"* for a total of ten "wants" between the two of you.

The key here is to initially focus on ten items that are of the utmost importance. These ten items become the foundation for designing a financial plan geared toward accomplishing your goals. A financial plan is much more important and meaningful to people who establish goals based on concrete examples, as opposed to accumulating money with no particular purpose in mind.

Working on your "wants" list is a wonderful mental exercise; very enlightening and a great deal of fun.

Concept #5

Establishing the Long-Term Perspective

The long-term perspective is not only important, it is critical to establishing an effective financial program. Many investments, such as stocks or mutual funds will fluctuate in value. There will be good times when you may tend to believe your investment can do nothing wrong. Your portfolio keeps increasing month after month. But there will be other times when it looks like you can do nothing right because the value of your investments seem to keep declining. These ups and downs are nothing to panic about; they are part of the overall cycle. It is the trend that you should be most concerned with versus the daily or monthly activity.

Questions to consider when reviewing your investment portfolio are:

* Given a reasonable period of time (three to five years or longer), is your portfolio increasing in value?

* Has your portfolio been increasing in an amount consistent with what you would consider reasonable?

* Is your portfolio keeping pace with the projections in your financial plan?

* Is your portfolio helping you to achieve your long-term goals?

Investing can be like a roller coaster ride. How fast that roller coaster goes up or goes down can be directly related to the type of portfolio you establish. Seeking assistance from a professional can help you design an investment portfolio that is compatible with the level of volatility and risk you are willing to accept.

the level of volatility and risk you are willing to accept.

Remember: your financial plan is like a road map. Use it to monitor your financial progress. Regularly compare the direction your portfolio is heading to that of your final destination. From time to time corrections will be in order, but do not make emotional, knee-jerk reactions. Altering your financial plan is an important decision. Give any course corrections careful thought. Finally, keep the long-term perspective.

Concept #6

Never Gamble with Your Future

A well-designed financial program evaluates the various risks you could encounter along your path to achieving financial security. Some of those risks are minor and others can be very significant. Whenever possible you should reduce or eliminate risks which can have a major impact on your ability to achieve your ultimate goals.

One of the best ways to accomplish this is to transfer some or all of that risk to someone else. When referring to problems like death, disability or serious illness, the best way to transfer that risk is through insurance companies. With proper analysis, evaluation, and plan design, you can usually acquire most or all of the needed insurance protection within a reasonable budget. This is where a professional advisor can show you all the options and formulate a custom strategy to satisfy your financial objectives.

There is no excuse for taking risks when you don't have to, especially if those risks can destroy your financial security.

Remember: "Gambling is creating a risk where none previously existed." This concept emphasizes the point that risks, like death and disability, already exist and you are gambling with your future if you do not take action to protect yourself.

Concept #7

The Only Guarantee in Life is that Everything Involves Risk

When developing an investment portfolio, it's more important to focus your attention on your risk tolerance level, rather than on the desired return. You should try to determine the amount of volatility or fluctuation in an investment portfolio you are willing to accept.

For example, assume you had a portfolio worth $100,000 and in one month the portfolio value dropped to $90,000 because of the market changes. How would this change affect you? Would you consider it a temporary fluctuation? Would you view this market change as a possible buying opportunity? Or would you be concerned that the market was going to crash? Would you want to pull your money out and run for the hills?

It is far more likely that the portfolio will fluctuate at a level beyond your risk tolerance if you try to achieve maximum returns with no consideration for the related risked involved.

You have to know and understand your risk tolerance in order to help yourself maintain a long-term perspective. If your portfolio's ups and downs are within your comfort level, the possibility of panicking and making rash decisions is minimized. Keeping your portfolio optimized will be based on the level of risk you are willing to take versus the amount of gain you wish to achieve. Understanding your risk tolerance level will help you select the appropriate mix of investments that you can live with, and, just as important, investments that won't keep you up all night with worry.

❖　　　❖　　　❖

Concept #8

Are You a Lender or an Investor?

The main point of this particular concept is to help people realize that equity-type investments typically offer the greatest rewards. They should not be approached with an irrational fear simply because they do not have a built-in guarantee.

Do you prefer to have your money in time certificates, money market accounts or passbook savings? Do you avoid investments like stocks, bonds or mutual funds? Understanding this concept may cause you to rethink your investment strategy.

Remember: The only reason somebody is guaranteeing you a fixed rate of return is because they are confident of earning a significantly higher percentage of return than they are willing to pay you. The difference of even a few percentage points over 10, 15 or 20 years could cost you tens or hundreds of thousands of dollars in lost income.

Even the most conservative individuals should consider incorporating some equity investments into their portfolio. Repositioning as little as 10 percent of your investments may add a little greater risk, but its overall impact on your portfolio could outweigh the possible loss by the long-term potential gains. There are numerous asset allocation strategies available that can maximize your investment return within your risk comfort level.

Each type of investment has its own advantages and disadvantages. Knowledge is key to choosing an appropriate asset mix. Seeking professional advice can assist when orchestrating a portfolio that will be balanced toward your particular investment objectives.

Concept #9

Know the Rules before You Play the Game

There are many government laws and regulations that can impact how your money is taxed, as you accumulate it, transfer it, and distribute it at the time of your death. These outside factors are the "rules of the game" and can significantly impact your ability to accumulate and retain your wealth.

All this may seem cumbersome and complicated, but it is a relatively easy matter to resolve. It just takes a little effort on your part. Seek the appropriate advisors such as, an estate attorney, an accountant and a financial planner. They can help you coordinate the right documents to make certain that your family does not pay any more in taxes than are absolutely necessary.

This concept emphasizes the need for some pre-emptive planning. You have to prepare for events that may be years in the future or could happen tomorrow. Many people put off this important step in their planning because they think there is always time to prepare the paperwork tomorrow. While some of these people may eventually do the necessary planning before it is too late, other procrastinators won't be as lucky.

Hopefully the examples described in Chapter 12 show the importance of having a professional review of the estate and income tax laws as an ongoing part of your financial plan. They should be reviewed on a regular basis to make certain there have not been significant changes that could adversely affect your financial security.

The government gives you a variety of ways to retain your assets. However, if you do not take advantage of the rules and regulations, the laws assume you would rather give the government a major portion of your estate instead of your spouse or children. A little bit of preparation and planning could go a long way to saving thousands or hundreds of thousands of dollars in your estate.

❖   ❖   ❖

Concept #10

If I Tell You Where it Hurts, Do I Still Have to Pay You?

Many times people feel they can accomplish most of their investment planning by themselves and save the fees that would otherwise go to an advisor. This can be a very shortsighted approach, since the fees are usually modest compared to the professional expertise made available to them. Quite often, fees are more than offset by the losses that one would incur through trial and error.

This concept is not saying that you absolutely must have an advisor, an accountant or an attorney. However, it is recommending that you speak to the professionals in their respective areas so you can better understand what they can do for you, and their related costs. Most professionals are happy to offer an initial consultation with no obligation or fee. After you interview one or more advisors you will be better informed about their services and be able to make a more intelligent decision as to whether you should hire him or her, or feel confident enough to proceed yourself.

Appendix

Benchmark Indexes

What is a "Benchmark Index"?

A "benchmark index" gives the investor a point of reference for evaluating a fund's performance. The S&P 500 is a commonly used basic benchmark for equity-oriented funds, including asset allocation, blanced funds, multi-asset global, and the Lehman Brothers Aggregate Bond Index (an overall bond benchmark) as the benchmark index for fixed-income funds, including convertible, high-yield and world-bond funds.

There are a number of secondary, specialized benchmarks. These benchmarks tend to give a better performance representation when trying to give an asset class category that approximates the investment mix in the benchmark. Because the S&P 500 is composed almost entirely of large-cap domestic stocks, it is good performance the overall market, but other comparisons are less useful. Comparing a foreign stock fund with the S&P 500, for example, does not tell the reader how the fund has done relative to foreign stock markets. Therefore, a fund's total return should be compared against one or more of the following indexes:

The following is a list of some of the most commonly referred to market indexes:

FB H-Y Bond (First High-Yield Index)

This index tracks the returns of all new publicly offered debt of more than $75 million rated below BBB.

JSE Gold (Johannesburg Stock Exchange Gold Index)

This index tracks the performance of gold-related companies o the Johannesburg Stock Exchange. The majority of these are gold mining stocks.

LB Agg (Lehman Brothers Aggregate Bond Index)

This is a combination of the Lehman brothers Government, Corporate, Mortgage-Backed, and Asset-backed Securities Indexes.

LB AHM (Lehman Brothers Adjustable-Rate Mortgage Index)

This index serves as a benchmark for the performance of adjustable-rate mortgage securities issued by GNMA, PNMA and PHLMC.

LB Corp (Lehman Brothers Government Bond Index)

This index tracks the returns of U.S. Treasuries, agency bonds, and 1- to 3-year U.S. government obligations.

LB Int (Lehman Brothers Intermediate-Term Treasury)

This index tracks the performance of U.S. Treasury Bonds with maturities up to 10 years.

LB L-T (Lehman Brothers Long-Term Treasury Index)

This index measures the returns of U.S. Treasury Bonds with maturities greater than ten years.

LB Mtg (Lehman Brothers Mortgage-Backed Securities Index)

This index includes 15- and 30-year fixed-rate securities backed by mortgage pools issued by GNMA, FNMA, and FHLMC.

LB Muni (Lehman Brothers Municipal Bond Index)

This index serves as a benchmark for the performance of long-term investment-grade, tax-exempt municipal bonds.

MSAllCtry (Morgan Stanley Capital International All Country Index)

This index tracks the performance of stock markets in 43 countries, including the united states and Japan.

MSCI EASEA (Morgan Stanley Capital International Europe, Australia and South-East Asia)

This index represents all the countries in the MSCI EAFE index minus japan.

MSCI EAFE (Morgan Stanley Capital International Europe, Australia, and Far East Index)

Widely accepted as a benchmark for international stock performance, the EAFE index is a market-wieghted aggregate of 20 individual country indexes that collectively represent many of the major markets of the world, excluding CANADA and United States.

MSCI Emerging (Morgan Stanley Capital International Emerging Markets)

This index is composed of 20 of the world's emerging markets: Argentina, Brazil, Chile, Colombia, Greece, India, Indonesia, Jordan, Korea, Malaysia, Mexico, Pakistan, Peru, the Philippines, Portugal, Sri Lanka, Taiwan, Thailand, Turkey, and Venezuela.

MSCI Europe (Morgan Stanley Capital Internal Europe Index)

This index measures the performance of stock markets in Austria, Belgium, Denmark, Finland, France, Germany, Ireland, Italy, the Netherlands, Norway, Spain, Sweden, Switzerland, and the United Kingdom.

MSCIFE ex Japan (Morgan Stanley Capital International Far East Index ex Japan)

This is an index of far Eastern markets, excluding Japan.

MSCI Japan (Morgan Stanley Capital International Japan Index)

This index measures the performance of Japan's stock market.

MSCI Latin Am (Morgan Stanley Capital International Latin America Index)

This index tracks the performance of Latin American markets.

MSCI PaciWe (Morgan Stanley Capital International PaciWe Index)

This index measures the performance of stock markets in Australia Hong Kong, Japan, New Zealand, Singapore and Malaysia.

MSCI World (Morgan Stanley Capital International World Index)

This index measures the performance of stock markets in 22 nations, including: Australia, Hong Kong, Germany, the United Kingdom, Canada, and the United States..

NSWdxUs (Morgan Stanley Capital International World Index ex U.S.)

This index follows the performance of stock markets in 21 countries excluding the United States.

Russell 2000

This commonly cited small-cap index tracks the returns of the smallest 2,000 firms in the Russell 3000 Index, which is composed of the 3,000 largest companies in the United states, as measured by market capitalization.

SB World (Salomom Brothers Non-U.S.-Dollar World Government Bond Index)

This index measures total-return performance of government bonds with a maturity of one year or more in 12 countries other than the United States. The index weighs bonds based on market capitalization, so that large debt-issuing countries such as JapAn and Germany have larger representations than do smaller issuing countries.

S&P 500 (Standard and Poor's 500 Index)

Often considered a surrogate for the overall market, this index is comprised of 400 industrial, 20 transpotation, 40 utility, and 40 financial companies.

S&P MidCap 400 (Standard and Poor's Mid-Cap 400 Index)

This index measures the performance of the largest 400 stocks outside of the S&) 500. These companies have market values ranging from $85 million to $7.16 billion.

Wil 4500 (Wilshire 4500 Index)

This index measures the performance of 4500 of the largest U.S. common-stock securities, excluding those in the S&P 500.

Wil 5000 (Wilshire 5000 Index)

This is an index of 500 of the largest U.S. stocks, determined by market capitalization. One of the broadest indexes, the Wilshire 5000 measures the performance of U.S. common stocks.

Wil REIT (Wilshire Real-Estate Investment Trust Index)

This is an index of real-estate investment trusts.

**Source: Principia for Mutual Funds, Morningstar, Inc.,
Chicago, IL – 312-424-4288**

Recommended Reading

There are a number of good books available that provide a more technical understanding of the different types of investments, as well as various investment strategies. The books listed below represent only a small number of resources available today. I strongly recommend that you go to your local library or bookstore and randomly browse through the finance and investment sections. This way you will be able to get a feel for the different ways authors try to convey their information. You will find that some books may be too technical, while others maintain your attention. Trying to educate yourself on investments can be difficult, especially if you try to read technical books that put you to sleep.

You should also consider subscribing to one or more financial publications, such as:

The Wall Street Journal

Barron's

Fortune magazine

Investor's Daily Newspaper

Worth Magazine

This is not intended to be a complete list of all the good newspapers or magazines, but it is a start.

Recommended Books:

Beating the Street by Peter Lynch, Simon & Schuster

Focusing Your Unique Ability by Dan Sullivan, The Strategic Coach 1-800-387-3206

The Great Crossover by Dan Sullivan, The Strategic Coach, 1-800-387-3206

How the Best Get Better by Dan Sullivan, The Strategic Coach 1-800-387-3206

Investment Policy by Charles D. Ellis, Irwin Professional Publishing

Money Dynamics for the 1990's by Venita VanCaspel, Simon and Schuster

One Up on Wall Street by Peter Lynch, Simon & Schuster

Pay Yourself First by Timothy W. Cunningham & Clay B. Mansfield, John Wiley & Sons, Inc.

Preserving Family Wealth Using Tax Magic by Richard W. Duff, Berkeley Press

The Warren Buffett Way by Robert G. Hagestrom, Jr., John Wiley & Sons, Inc.

Your Wealth Building Years by Adriane G. Berg, Newmarket Press